Serving in His Court

Biblical Principles for Personal Evangelism from the Heart of a Coach

Larry Stamm

As a pastor, this is easily one of the best books on personal evangelism I have ever read. As a believer who struggles just like everyone else in comfortably sharing your faith, it is an absolute must. Both the author's experience as a coach, and the heart that he has for God, His Kingdom, His Church and the world all come through in encouraging and challenging ways. The discussion of why we need the Gospel is worth the price of the book by itself! If you want a great book to use in a small group, or just want to be encouraged and coached in your own witness, you won't find a better book than this.

Tim Price, Pastor
Emmanuel Baptist Church
Kingsport, TN

I cannot think of anyone more qualified to write a "how to" on evangelism than Larry Stamm. He has a love for the gospel, the God who gave it, the Savior who bought it and the sinner who needs it. His heart and many years of experience sharing this gospel makes his voice one that needs to be heard on this most important subject.

Scott Watson, Pastor
Fellowship Baptist Church
Bluff City, TN

Larry Stamm knows his stuff and is an energetic, solid, effective communicator. You get substance with Larry in a way that is understandable, practical, and engaging.

Tom Oyler, Teaching Pastor
Grace Fellowship Church
Johnson City, TN

Larry Stamm is a passionate and gifted speaker who teaches from the overflow in his own life. When it comes to connecting with our Jewish roots as modern day Christians, no one can make the topic come alive like Larry. He will give you a fresh perspective on your faith that will inspire you to want to share it with others.

Dave McAuley, Founder
Summit Leadership Foundation
Johnson City, TN

Larry Stamm's teaching leaves the hearer longing to carry the Cross of Jesus The Messiah the extra mile. His understanding of the scripture preps your walk by washing your feet thoroughly with the Word and fitting you comfortably with the shoes of the Gospel of Peace.

Bill Edwards, Pastor
Freedom Fellowship
Rockaway Beach, New York

Larry was a fine teacher and motivator of our young ETSU tennis players. He helped them grow technically and emotionally in their competitive careers. But, more importantly, he was an outstanding mentor, influencing their values and life skills so that they could become mature and productive adults of character.

Dave Mullins, Tennis Coach and Athletic Director (Retired)
East Tennessee State University

Larry Stamm is real. When encouraging people to share their faith, rather than dealing with pie-in-the-sky theoreticals, Larry deals with realities. He doesn't tell you not to be afraid; he trains you to share Jesus through your fears. My group loved our time with Larry. Yours will, too.

Lindy Apon, Pastor
Parkway Baptist Church
Knoxville, TN

To every Christian who aspires to share their faith in Jesus.
You change eternity.

Acknowledgements

I want to thank my Lord and Savior Jesus, who is my life and in whom I live, breath and have my being. I want to thank my beautiful wife Lori, for being my best friend and greatest champion in ministry. Much thanks to Alton Gansky, my editor; Ken Raney, my graphic artist; and Jack Cavanaugh, my interior page designer. Their professional expertise and support was tremendous and helped make this project possible. Many thanks to my friends at Grace Fellowship Church in Johnson City, TN for their fellowship and support since 1993. Thanks also to my friends at Jews for Jesus, who have taught me so much about being a minister of the gospel. Finally, a big thank you to Daryl, Bruce, Dave, and Tim for their various contributions to this book.

Table of Contents

Preface

I like challenges. It's part of my nature and upbringing. My father exemplified the power of a healthy work ethic. Over the years, whether managing the rental units he owned, selling real estate or insurance, or managing his plastics company (which made plastic fruit and those old-style coin holders), he worked hard. On one occasion he said to me, "Kid, there are no free lunches. If you want something, work." And work I did. I got my first job when I was twelve delivering an afternoon paper in my Treasure Island, Florida neighborhood. I haven't stopped since. The challenge of developing and maintaining a work ethic also helped me as I immersed myself in sports during my growing up years.

Sports have always been my passion. I played lots of sports in my youth, but tennis was my competitive outlet. I began playing tennis at age nine when my mother took me to our local tennis club. At ten, I played my first tennis tournaments and excelled. I later earned a Florida state junior ranking. From age twelve to eighteen I played the junior circuit, earning my highest state ranking of #20 in the boys 16-under singles division.

Being a competitive athlete has its challenges.

I played one season of college tennis at West Virginia University in the spring of 1983 before transferring to the University of Florida where I quit competitive tennis. The challenge there was not in excelling, but dealing with failure—failure to play up to the standards I'd set for myself. I'll share more about that later.

After graduating from college I took a tennis coaching position at my high school coach's tennis academy in Seminole, Florida. Considering my options in the fall of 1986, I could either have pursued an entry-level position in the telecommunications industry or take this coaching position earning double what any entry level position could have paid. That was an easy choice. Tennis anyone?

Turns out I was well suited for this kind of career. I loved coaching and spent fourteen years working with players of every level—from little children who had never held a racquet to touring professionals whose livelihood depended on winning tennis matches.

Being Jewish and believing in Jesus also provides its own unique challenges.

I grew up in a Reform Jewish home, a liberal expression of Judaism, and attended a local synagogue. Our family was more socially and culturally connected to the Jewish community than spiritually connected to God. I had always believed in God and also believed He knew me and that I was special in His eyes. After my Bar Mitzvah (a ceremonial rite of passage where a Jewish boy becomes a man), I lost interest in my Judaism. Interestingly, I never stopped believing in God. In fact, I believed in God and thought He knew me. I believed I was special in His eyes. In high school, I focused on my classes and sports, thinking that I would find happiness by excelling in the classroom and on the tennis court.

But accomplishment didn't equal happiness. The more I tried to make myself happy through achieving, the more unhappy I became. In college people shared their faith in Jesus with me, but I didn't want to hear about it. As a Jewish young man, I was taught Jesus was the God of the Gentiles and wasn't for us. Still, the Holy Spirit kept working on me and people kept coming. In December 1987, I became a believer in Jesus as my Messiah, Lord, and Savior.

I'm a product of marketplace evangelism. I refer to the "marketplace" as anywhere outside the walls of a church building. My journey to faith came through the personal evangelistic efforts of individuals like you—individuals God used to bring me to Himself. I didn't attend a Bible study or church service, watch a Christian TV program, listen to Christian radio, or talk with a pastor, priest, or rabbi. Rather, it was ordinary people in the marketplace sharing the gospel that brought me to God.

At the University of Florida in 1984, a friend named Greg (some of the names in this book have been changed) shared his faith with me. He said, "Larry, there's absolute truth and you can get in touch with it." Then he posed a series of questions that rocked my world: "Do you know where you came from? Do you know who you are? And do you know where you're going when you die?" I didn't know how to answer. It sent me spiraling into an existential crisis of sorts. I didn't know who I was, and I certainly didn't know where I was going when I died. I was a person walking in quiet desperation. I knew I was lost, but had no idea if there was a found. I started searching for truth. I neither embraced my Judaism, nor accepted Christianity, but I began to consciously search for truth. Then came Herb, the TV advertising professional...

In the summer of 1986, just prior to my graduation from college, I spent a six week internship at an ABC television affiliate in Gainesville, Florida, learning the ins and outs of selling on-air advertising time. As a telecommunications major, I thought it would be good to learn about advertising. Turns out Herb, my professional mentor that summer, also spent much of our time together telling me about Jesus. We spent many an hour in his car going from sales appointment to sales appointment, so there was ample opportunity to talk about spiritual things. Finally, there was the traveling insurance salesman I met on an airplane...

It was early September 1987 and I was flying from Atlanta to St. Petersburg where I was living. On the airplane I met a gentleman named Steve. I was reading *The Story of Philosophy* by historian Will Durant. Steve looked at me and said, "Are you interested in philosophy?"

Straightening my back with pride, I said, "Yes, yes I am." The truth was I was just dabbling.

He beamed. "Great, I have a masters degree in philosophy. We have a lot to talk about." He did most of the talking. "You tell me you're Jewish and you believe in God?"

"Yes."

"Well why don't you ask God as you know Him— Ask the God of Abraham, Isaac, and Jacob to show you the truth about Jesus. Ask the

God of Israel to show you if Jesus is the Messiah, and He will."

He encouraged me to get a Bible since I had never read the New Testament. He wrote some Scripture references on his business card and told me to call if I wanted, then he said he would be praying for me.

I got off the plane that afternoon and prayed a deep theological prayer. "God, help." Can you relate? I added, "God, I don't know about Jesus, the Bible, or Christianity, but if Jesus is the Messiah, show me.

Three months later, after reading the New Testament for the first time and asking God to reveal the truth about Jesus, God answered my prayer. In December of 1987, God showed me Jesus was and is the Messiah, that He died for my sins and rose again from the dead, and that through faith in Him, I could be forgiven, know God personally, and experience the abundant and eternal life He promises.

That was not the end, but rather the beginning.

Since that time, God has given me a heart for people, a passion for the gospel, and a love for His Church. As a professional tennis coach at clubs and academies in Florida, and as an Assistant Tennis Coach at East Tennessee State University, the tennis court was a great platform for sharing God's Good News.

From 1997-1999, I played guitar and sang with the *Liberated Wailing Wall*, the mobile evangelistic music team of Jews for Jesus, a missions organization reaching out to the Jewish people. I also served as a vocational missionary with the same organization in New York City from 2003-2009. During that time, I had the opportunity to share the gospel in a myriad of ways. Our music team did over 500 presentations during our tour, and as a missionary, I had the privilege of speaking in churches 40-50 times per year.

For over six years I ministered to my Jewish people in New York City. I also did public outreach in other big cities and on college campuses around the world. I engaged in hundreds of witnessing conversations with people from various backgrounds.

In my personal and professional life, I've shared the gospel every which way possible: in homes, cafés, apartments, on tennis and basketball courts, in vans traveling to and from tennis matches and tournaments, on street corners, via email, in letters, door to door, and outside arenas and stadiums.

This book, however, is not about street ministry. Rather it's a book about personal evangelism, and personal evangelism takes place in the context of relationships. This book is about where you and I live. We have family, friends, associates, coworkers, baristas, and other people we know in our groups, leagues, organizations, associations—all part of our regular sphere of influence.

A recent Pew Survey[1] on religion found one-in-five Americans identify religiously as "none"—meaning they have no religious affiliation. That's 60 million Americans and that number grows daily. Additionally, another survey found 20% of all people living in North America do not know a Christian "personally." While those numbers are stunning, they only reflect a portion of the spiritual need. Regardless of whether anyone in your sphere of influence fits one of these categories, there are people in your life who need the Lord.

I believe the gospel goes forth most comprehensively through the testimony of the individual as they share in their sphere of influence. I see a great need in today's Church for believers to be encouraged and equipped to engage the world around them.

I don't know about your experience, but I would characterize personal evangelism as challenging. Whatever your involvement, my prayer is that God will use this book as a tool for you to grow in your Christian life—grow closer to God, grow a bigger heart for the lost, and grow in becoming a more faithful witness to others.

Whether you hear the word "evangelism" and shudder, or have lots of personal evangelistic experience, there is room to grow. For our Christian life is dynamic and none of us ever "arrives."

This book is a humble submission to my Lord and Savior, Jesus. I pray He might multiply it for His Glory and Kingdom Purpose as He multiplied the loaves and fishes in feeding people.

Introduction

To everything there is a season,
a time for every purpose under heaven.
Ecclesiastes 3:1

This is a book about principles and process in the area of personal evangelism.

As a fulltime professional tennis coach for fourteen years, I understand the importance of principles and process. Growing as a tennis player includes understanding and applying the principles for success—this is a process.

As witnesses for Jesus, when we better understand biblical principles for personal evangelism and apply them, our witness will grow. This is also a process.

Why biblical principles? Because, "Faith comes by hearing and hearing by the Word of God" (Romans 10:17). This is true for the Christian and for those whom they care about who've not yet met Christ.

And what is the end game of this process? That you would become better equipped and more encouraged to engage the process of personal evangelism under the leading of the Holy Spirit.

Serving in His Court

Jesus said, "For even the Son of Man did not come to be served, but to serve, and to give His life a ransom for many" (Mark 10:45). Jesus entered the court of this world to serve His Father. We as followers of Jesus are also called to serve and give. In the evangelistic endeavor serving and giving includes praying for people, loving them in Jesus name, serving them through good deeds, and proclaiming the gospel message, the one message that saves.

Serving in His Court is a motif that is relevant to the evangelistic endeavor. I like sports. You could call me a big fan, particularly of the Gator and Yankee persuasion. We as believers are part of a team, the body of Christ, the Church. We're all in this game of life together. In fact, we're all called to fulfill our roles on the team, playing our part in the game.

For our purpose I will use the tennis court as a picture of our world and you and I as servants (players) on the team (His Church). Jesus has an agenda. This Kingdom building agenda is called the Great Commission and all Christians are called to participate. Our participation is to be witnesses of the King to the very ends of the world (the Court).

Whether you like tennis or not, I hope you find the motif engaging and enjoyable. You may even learn some things about tennis you never knew. Ultimately, my hope is this motif will help you better understand and engage the evangelistic process for His glory, our good, and for the blessing of those we will serve in Jesus' name.

Simple Yet Profound and Important

When we understand and engage the principles found in God's Word, we'll glorify Him and become an effective witness. "And also if anyone competes in athletics, he is not crowned unless he competes according to the rules" (2 Timothy 2:5).

This is a simple book to be sure. We will cover all the main tenets of personal evangelism. Certainly there are many books devoted specifically to many of the individual chapter topics discussed. So I would encourage you to continue your process of growing in your witness through more reading.

If the concept of personal evangelism is a bit intimidating, this is certainly the book for you. If you've "been there and done that," having had many personal witnessing encounters, you will still find this book a useful tool. Don't confuse my simple approach with unimportance. Sometimes the simplest component is the most essential one.

While coaching at East Tennessee State University in the mid-1990s, I was doing an individual workout with Sonny, one of our team members. Sonny was a strapping 6'5" Englishman and one of our starting players. He was gifted with excellent eye hand coordination. Sonny nicknamed me "Lazarus" or "Laz." I've been called lots of names in my life, but never that one.

At the beginning of our workout Sonny said he wasn't hitting the ball cleanly with his forehand groundstroke. Something was amiss and he couldn't figure it out. So I took my shopping cart full of tennis balls to the side of the court opposite Sonny, and began feeding him balls, analyzing his swing as he struck forehand after forehand from the baseline.

Tennis coaches hit thousands of balls to players and watch their technique, analyzing every part of the player's stroke. This can be mundane and monotonous, but a trained eye can identify the issue and help solve the problem.

At first glance everything about Sonny's swing looked good. His footwork looked good too. Then I watched his eyes as I hit a few balls his direction. Voila! Just as he was about to make contact with the ball Sonny was looking up over the net. He was taking his eye off the ball a split second before contact, causing him to hit the ball off the racquet's center and away from the "sweet spot."

I advised Sonny to see the ball all the way through the hitting zone. He began hitting the ball true time after time. He shouted over the net, "Lazarus, you're a genius."

I don't know about that, but I appreciated the comment. You see, watching the ball is essential to properly hitting a tennis ball, regardless of the level of tennis you play. If you're not a tennis player, apply the principle to any sport requiring you to watch the object you're striking.

The moral of the story is this: the basics are essential to success no matter where you are in the process. In the area of personal evangelism, there are essentials that, if overlooked, can trip up anyone—even the experts.

The Great Commission is Not Optional

People are broken. People need the Lord. Jesus is the answer. That's why the Lord came to die for our sins and rise again. He came to restore that broken relationship between God and man that sin's curse brought. He's called His people, the Church, to be ambassadors of reconciliation. The Great Commission serves as our marching orders.

At the heart of the Great Commission is Jesus' command to "go out into all nations and make disciples" (Matthew 28:19). God's Kingdom building program requires His children, you and me, to proclaim the gospel of Jesus Christ, for, as we saw earlier, ". . . faith comes by hearing and hearing by the word of God" (Romans 10:17). People need to trust in Christ to be forgiven of sin, to experience the abundant and eternal life Jesus promises, and to go to heaven.

When it comes to evangelism, we all will struggle with heart, commitment, and initiative issues. Why? Because we are in a spiritual war. Yet Jesus has achieved the victory. He said He would build His Church and the gates of Hades would not prevail against it. Our God gives us the privilege of participating with Him—or "co-laboring" if you will—in His Kingdom building program called the Great Commission. What a blessing.

This Won't be Easy (But it's Doable and Worthwhile)

I like physical training. I've been working out since my youth. But to be honest, I also like when a workout is completed. The satisfaction I derive includes all the immediate benefits of a relaxed mind and body, and longer-term benefits such as the decreased risk of various health problems. A physical training routine is also a huge victory in another way: it is victory over laziness.

Personal evangelism is like personal fitness training. If I did it when I felt like it, I wouldn't do it very often. This sentiment is echoed by the late baseball star Satchel Paige, who said, "I don't generally like running. I believe in training by rising gently up and down from the bench."

Engaging the evangelistic process is a commitment rather than a feeling. When we take the initiative, step out in faith, and share the good news of Jesus in word and deed, it's not only a personal spiritual victory for us, it blesses others and blesses the heart of God.

Make no mistake. Personal evangelism is work, perhaps the most critical work this side of heaven. Think about it. It's one thing on earth we won't be able to do in heaven. Worship in heaven will be perfect. Fellowship will also be perfect in heaven. We'll serve God perfectly in heaven and enjoy the process completely. Evangelism, however, is something done in the here and now. But it ain't easy.

Our son Elijah enjoys playing basketball and when he first joined a league, I was the team's coach. Prior to the season I took him to the basketball court to practice. As he shot, it took all the energy his nine year-old body could muster just to get the ball near the basket. Making a shot was another matter. He continued to miss and soon grew frustrated. I gently stopped him and smiled. "Son, did you really think this was going to be easy?" The truth and the humor in that moment disarmed and encouraged him. He knew that I knew...and even though it didn't necessarily make it any easier physically, in some way it eased his burden.

I wonder if our Heavenly Father feels the same regarding our engagement of personal evangelism. "Did you really think this was going to be easy?" Change is hard, growing is hard. I suppose that's why growing pains are well—painful.

The pain of growing in grace, growing in our witness, and in so doing, growing closer to our Lord through personal evangelism is of utmost importance—and it's a pain that brings great gain for the Kingdom of God and in our own lives.

The benefits of physical exercise are countless. We're relaxed, renewed, and in some way the exertion makes us stronger. The pouring out of ourselves fills us up. Yes, that's a paradox. I'm reminded of a statement Jesus made in John 4 that I've pondered many times in my Christian life.

In this passage Jesus had just ministered to the Samaritan woman at the well. The disciples urged Jesus to eat (John 4:32). He answered with a remarkable statement: "My food is to do the will of Him who sent Me, and to finish His work" (John 4:34). Spiritually, I can say that I have experienced great joy in my life when I've stepped out in faith and shared the gospel with people. Frankly, that joy isn't in the response of the audience, but rather in doing what God has called me to do. I relate to that Scripture. I've often felt fed by God in doing evangelism. I've been filled up as I pour myself out for Him.

The Win

Many believers want to engage in personal evangelism, yet feel discouraged and ill-equipped. The goal of this book is to provide biblically-based principles that will encourage and equip you to more effectively share Jesus with those whom you come into contact, whether in your family, a neighbor, a coworker, or even a stranger as you "witness on the way."

And what will be the win? Well, others will be blessed, the heart of God will be blessed, and you and I will grow closer to the Lord in the process. Now that's what I call victory!

As Christian writer Bill Bright says in his book, *Witnessing without Fear*: "Success in witnessing is simply taking the initiative to share Christ in the power of the Holy Spirit, and leaving the results to God."[2]

So wherever you are on your faith journey, today begins a new season in the area of personal evangelism. Today brings a new day filled with new challenges, new opportunities, and new blessings. Shall we begin?

Part 1—Understanding The Game

Chapter 1

The Rules

And also if anyone competes in athletics, he is not crowned unless he competes according to the rules.
2 Timothy 2:5

American tennis professional Andy Roddick, a perennial world top ten player between 2002-2010, was known for his blistering serve. He could hit the serve over 150 mph. I was in Cincinnati in 2002 for a professional tennis tournament and had a chance to see that serve up close. Roddick was practicing on center court the day before the tournament began. I was just behind the court when he began practicing serves—in my direction. My friends and I had to duck a few times as balls came whizzing past us.

One of the highlights of Roddick's career occurred in 2003 when, as a 21 year-old, he won his only Grand Slam Tournament, the US Open. That was in September. He attained the World #1 ranking the following November.

His rise to stardom came with great commitment, perseverance, patience, and some real obstacles. At age seventeen Roddick almost quit competitive tennis after experiencing a losing streak on the junior circuit. His coach encouraged him to focus on the game for a few more months before hanging up the racquet for good. Roddick stuck with it and the rest, as they say, is history.

Andy Roddick's journey as a professional tennis player illustrates "the rules" of engagement for a tennis player, or any athlete. Those rules include: playing tennis is a process, it's a heart issue, and it's a team thing.

No one decides to play tennis and the next day, week, or month wakes up a good tennis player. Becoming proficient involves understanding that it's a process. It takes time. So does evangelism.

Tennis is about the heart. It takes a heart commitment to learn, grow, and develop. There will be obstacles along your journey. For Andy Roddick, it was facing a losing streak. Yet he made a heart commitment to continue and overcome. As we'll see, personal evangelism requires a heart commitment too. We know there will be many obstacles in our path to sharing the gospel with others. Commitment will get us over those obstructions.

Finally, tennis is a team thing. We may think of tennis as an individual sport. Yet, the reality is there is always a team behind the athlete. There are coaches who teach, family who encourages and supports, practice partners, and other athletes on a similar path. In fact, at the professional level, there is what is known as the "entourage." The entourage may include the coach, hitting partner, fitness guru, sports psychologist, nutritionist, massage therapist, agent, and others. Personal evangelism is also a team thing. We, the Church, are engaging the Great Commission together—with God and with one another.

Understanding these three "rules" of engagement, these overarching principles, will serve us well as we think about our effort in reaching the lost for Jesus Christ. They are: 1) evangelism is a process; 2) evangelism is a heart issue; and 3) evangelism is a team thing.

For if we don't get these straight, our efforts will be hampered. When we engage the world with these in mind, our experience will be more satisfying, our relationship with God will grow deeper, and our service to others will be more effective.

Evangelism is a Process

As a college tennis coach I would at times share this pearl of wisdom with our tennis team: "Guys, winning is not an event, it's a process."

You know, winning a match, winning a tournament, winning at anything generally takes a commitment—a commitment to the process. In tennis, the decision to commit and the initiative to follow through are essential for success. The practice. Running. Lifting. The competition. Losing. Learning. Sometimes more losing and more learning. Learning how to compete, how to win, how to handle situations and experiences. All of it brings an individual or team to the moment of culmination—that moment in time when it all comes together.

But through it all it's the process that matters. Sometimes processes are productive, sometimes not so much. Success in life is often the combination of processes we engage in and the decisions we make. It's true in athletics, it's true in life, and it's true in the court of the evangelistic endeavor, our world.

Evangelism is a process, not an event. Paradoxically, the process is made up of separate events which God uses in an individual's journey to faith. And how God brings people to Himself is infinite in variety. "God has created each individual in His likeness, and He is a God who delights in diversity; so there is an infinite number of ways His image can be expressed. Just as each person is unique, so the way in which God draws each person to Himself is also unique. Every Christian has a story to tell."[3]

Jesus' parable of the soils (Luke 8:4-15, Matthew 13:1-23, Mark 4:1-20) sheds light on this reality. We're called to sow gospel seed, which is the Word of God, and that takes time. The soil is the condition of a human heart, as Jesus explained, and is where the seed lands. As one Bible commentator notes, "The soils do not represent individual moments of decision as much as a lifelong response to God's Word."[4]

Think about it in the physical. A farmer sows seed—that's an event. It rains one day—that's another event. The sun comes up day after day and feeds that seed—those days are individual events. It rains another day—that's an event. And so on.

The first time I heard the gospel, I was in college. My initial responses were outright rejection of that message. However, people kept coming, and the Holy Spirit kept working on my heart. Four years passed between the time people began witnessing to me in 1983 and the day I trusted in Christ in 1987.

By understanding evangelism is a process, you will gain confidence and be able to balance the urgency of sharing Jesus while respecting people enough to give them time, space, and margins to process the truth.

Years ago, I was at Brooklyn College in New York City talking to students about Jesus. I was sharing the gospel with an orthodox Jewish student and I asked him, "Have you ever heard this message before?" Perplexed, he said, "Never in my life." He certainly needed time to process the gospel message.

We don't know the condition of a human heart and we may not know a person's previous exposure to a Christian witness. But God does. Yet, God calls us to engage and sow gospel seed, the Word of God, believing in God to do what only He can do—bless our efforts. We also sow and 'water' seed through prayer and good works, which we'll discuss later. But whatever and however we sow, it is God alone who brings the increase. The Apostle Paul wrote, "I planted, Apollos watered, but God gave the increase" (1 Corinthians 3:6-7). The same is true for us.

In the spring and summer of 2013, my wife Lori and our two children, Elijah and Shoshanna, and I, tried gardening for the first time. Biting into our first spring onion was thrilling. We learned about the process of gardening. When you garden you have to plant seeds at the right time, you have to water just enough, you have to tend your garden regularly, and you have to believe that your hard work will yield a harvest.

Giving too much information too soon, sharing all your biblical knowledge and everything you know about Jesus and the gospel is counterproductive. It's possible to nullify seed that's been sown. A reasonable amount of water is necessary for growth as in a light summer shower or controlled watering. But a deluge from a big storm or a fire hydrant will wash the seed away. That same garden that provided us delicious spring onions in the springtime, washed out in an East Tennessee summer rain. Water is good. Too much water—not so much.

We shouldn't overdo the process, unload everything we know and share it in one sitting. Instead, we sow and water as the Holy Spirit leads, while leaving the results to God. In general, people who trust in Christ typically need several exposures to the gospel message before believing in Him.

Because if people are spiritually thirsty; we shouldn't usher them to a fire hydrant. Rather, give them a refreshing cool cup of water. Respecting the process will allow people to process and move toward Jesus as they're exposed to biblical truth.

While a missionary in New York City, I was working with a Jewish man named David, an elderly man who had a scientific background. He was an agnostic engineer with no religious upbringing. He wasn't sure God existed but he was curious. I worked with David for a year, meeting him once or twice a month. I shared Scripture with him, in addition to articles and books that provided evidence of God's existence. Along the way I challenged him to pray a "seekers prayer": "God, if you're real, please reveal Yourself to me." I have found it a good way to share with the agnostic, the seeker, and even the cynic or skeptic. After a year of periodic meetings, I was at David's house in Queens one afternoon. He said, "Larry, I've come to a place where I believe in God." That was huge. From there I proceeded to share the truth claims of Jesus. When I left New York City, David still hadn't trusted in Christ, but he was definitely moving toward the light of Messiah Jesus.

Even Paul, though saved in a moment on the Damascus Road, heard the gospel in Acts 8 from Stephen's testimony even as he consented to Stephen's stoning. Paul's persecution of the church wasn't due to lack of gospel understanding but rather because of it. He simply rejected the truth until his conversion in Acts 9. There may have been believers who tried to share with Paul and who may have even been praying for his salvation. For Jesus said, "Pray for those who spitefully use you and persecute you" (Matthew 5:44).

Every person is on a journey, including you and me. And evangelism is a process. So enjoy the journey, understand the process, and trust in the Lord as you sow and water—leaving the results to God.

Evangelism is a Heart Issue

I remember it all too well: It was the spring of 1983, and I was a deeply discouraged 19 year-old college tennis player.

My freshman season didn't go so well. That January, I transferred from Florida's St. Petersburg Junior College to join the tennis team at West Virginia University (in the dead of winter). A former high school teammate was playing #1 singles on the team and had encouraged me to attend the university so I could play on the men's tennis team.

I envisioned joining the team and excelling. That's how it played out in my mind. The reality, however, was that I didn't adjust well. College tennis was new, playing indoors was new, and my one-handed backhand was new, as I had made a switch from two hands just six months earlier. I made the team, traveled and played in about a third of the matches that spring. But I didn't play anywhere near my expectations.

The coach wanted me to return for my sophomore year, but wasn't willing to give me any scholarship money. I felt discouraged and defeated. Earning a tennis scholarship was the reason I moved from Florida to West Virginia.

When I transferred to the University of Florida that fall, I was again encouraged by another friend from high school to try out for the tennis team as a walk on. He was playing for the Gators and wanted me on the team. I wasn't in the mood. I was burned out with tennis, disappointed with my performance on the West Virginia University team. Frankly, my heart was not into playing.

Any endeavor done with excellence, whether in athletics,

evangelism, or anything else, requires a heart in the right place. It is true for the spiritual life. "But sanctify Christ as Lord in your hearts, always being ready to make a defense to everyone who asks you to give an account for the hope that is in you, yet with gentleness and reverence" (1 Peter 3:15 NASB).

This verse packs a punch. The prerequisite for what we share and the spirit in which we share it requires that our hearts be in alignment with Christ who sits on the throne of our hearts.

Evangelism is a heart issue.

Central to God's redemptive plan is His heart's desire "to seek and save the lost" (Luke 19:10). "Lost" refers to you and me before our salvation experience. It also refers to those people we interact with daily in the marketplace, people who have yet to trust in Jesus.

The parable of the Lost Sheep in Luke 15 illustrates God's heart for the spiritually lost. In it, we see a picture of a shepherd taking the initiative to look for a missing sheep, searching until it is found. Upon finding it the shepherd rejoices. This beautiful picture illustrates God as the Initiator who seeks out sinners and feels great joy in their repentance. Jesus explains "there will be more joy in heaven over one sinner who repents than over ninety-nine just persons who need no repentance" (v. 7).

How about your heart and mine? Are we aligned with God's heart in His passion for the lost? Have we, in the area of our personal witness, sanctified or set apart "Christ as Lord in our hearts." Are we conscious that people need the Lord? Today, there are people in your sphere of influence that need Jesus. The reality is that "salvation is found in no one else, for there is no other name under heaven given among men by which we must be saved" (Acts 4:12).

The Apostle Paul is a prime example of one whose heart beat for the lost. In Romans 10:1, he wrote, "Brethren, my heart's desire and prayer to God for Israel is that they might be saved."

In Romans 9:13, Paul expressed the intensity of his heartbeat for the salvation of his Jewish people: "I tell the truth in Christ, I am not lying, my conscience also bearing me witness in the Holy Spirit, that I have great sorrow and continual grief in my heart. For I could wish that I myself were accursed from Christ for my brethren, my countrymen according to the flesh..."

Do you hear his fervor? Can you feel it?

A great place to begin growing a heartfelt desire for the lost is to surrender to the Lord in prayer, committing our witness and evangelistic endeavors to Him. Something along the lines of, "Lord, give me Your heart for the lost and give me the faith to follow You in this area of my life. Amen."

Once we've "set apart Christ as Lord," we will be more apt to go where He calls us to go, do what He calls us to do, and say what He would have us say to those with whom He calls us to share.

What does this look like in practice? What's the next step for you and for me? I don't know. But God does. Remember, when our heart is aligned with His, we should follow where He leads, walking by faith. When God called Abraham to go to a distant land sight unseen (Genesis 12), Abraham obeyed, leaving behind all he knew for an unknown destination God had promised to give him. When Jesus called His first disciples, He said only, "Follow me and I will make you fishers of men." He didn't explain what He meant. Still, they followed. When the Lord calls us to go and make disciples of all nations, the "going" looks different for you and for me. Yet the underlying principle of following remains the same: set apart Christ as Lord in your heart.

Wait. Can you hear it? That still small voice? It's the Lord and He's calling us to go. Go where? He'll show us later. For now, just take the next step with Him. What is that step? It is, "Yes, Lord." Remember, it's a heart thing.

Evangelism is a Team Thing

As you might have guessed, I'm a sports fan. The Florida Gators and New York Yankees are my favorite teams. Now you may not be a Gators or Yankees fan, and you might not even like sports, but there's an important principle from the sporting world that applies to Christians.

Teamwork is critical in team and individual sports. A common trait in award acceptance speeches given by champions of individual sports is the idea that their team helped achieve victory. In athletics it takes many people working together in order to accomplish the goal.

As it goes in the sporting arena, so it goes in the court of evangelism. For evangelism is a team thing. It is neither exclusively a "God thing," nor exclusively a "Me thing." Rather, evangelism is a "We thing."

As noted earlier, Jesus, at the beginning of His ministry, said to His disciples "Follow me and I will make you fishers of men" (Matthew 4:19). At the end of His ministry, just before ascending to heaven He stated, "Go and make disciples of all nations...and I will be with you always."

One of the mysteries of the gospel is that while God is all-powerful and is the author of salvation, He chooses to use people like you and me to bring others to Himself. For we, the church, are integral to His redemptive plan. In fact, the Lord commands us to be actively involved in His redemptive work.

The implication is that we can neither shirk our personal responsibility to witness, nor feel overwhelmed that we have to do the work of evangelism alone. Because God in His grace is sufficient to enable you and me to do our part in the evangelistic effort. The Apostle Paul wrote, "Not that we are sufficient of ourselves to think of anything as being from ourselves, but our sufficiency is from God, who also made us sufficient as ministers of the new covenant..." (2 Corinthians 3:5-6).

Additionally, in 1 Corinthians 12:12-21, Paul wrote that all believers are part of the body of Christ. That body is diverse and yet has a unity of purpose. You and I are all members of the same body, yet represent different parts. And we all have an important part to play in the function of the body.

While a missionary in New York City, I had occasion to witness to orthodox Jewish men. A few years later, while serving as the Local Outreach Pastor of my home church in Johnson City, TN, I received a call from a friend and former missionary associate from

Washington, DC. My friend Larry told me of a newly saved orthodox Jewish man he met while spending some time in New York City. Larry told me the man said to say hello to me. I had witnessed to him while I served in the Big Apple. When he told me the man's name, I didn't recognize it. I had no idea who he was talking with. It's interesting because I didn't have a personal ministry to many orthodox men and felt I should have remembered the man's name.

I tell that story to illustrate that my witness, even though I don't remember the person, was just one witness in the process. There would have been others who continued ministry to this gentleman along his journey of faith.

I praise God that he used me in the process of this man's journey. And it reminds me that I am one member of a very large team.

Think about your journey or that of someone you know who has come to faith in Jesus. I've mentioned several influential witnesses in my journey. Think about the team of servants God brought across your path or that someone else whose journey included touch points with several believers along the way.

This is a beautiful aspect of being a member of the team. No matter our role, we all get to rejoice in the victory, God's victory, as He ushers people into His Kingdom.

In late April 2002, our men's tennis team at East Tennessee State University was playing in the Southern Conference Tennis Tournament. Charleston, South Carolina, the tournament site, was experiencing record heat and it was brutal for all the teams. We had a very long semifinal match against the University of North Carolina, Greensboro, which took an immense amount of physical energy. We had been in the same situation the previous year, winning a very difficult semifinal match in hot weather and having to play for the championship the next day. The previous year we lost. You might say we were a bit wilted for the final.

Using massage, hydration and rest, our trainer did a phenomenal job to help the guys recover after that grueling semifinal match. Furman defeated us in last year's championship match. We hoped the result of this final would be different.

The next day we beat Furman (after having lost to them just weeks earlier) to win the Southern Conference Championship and advance to the NCAA Tournament. It was our best match of the year, as we overcame the sweltering heat and our arch-rival to claim the title!

It was a proud moment for the men's tennis team of East Tennessee State. And part of the backstory is the trainer for that weekend, a student himself at our school. He played a huge part in our being able to compete at a high level.

The point is this: all of us matter. In fact, God has roles for each of us. We are on the same team, the Church, and what we do matters, regardless of how big or small we may perceive our role to be.

I kidded the trainer after the victory, telling him he was our MVP, our Most Valuable Person. I was only half-kidding. Because without him we wouldn't have been physically ready to play championship caliber tennis.

You may think your contribution to God's redemptive plan is meager. Think again. You may not know how important your role is. You don't necessarily need to know the details, but you should know your effort matters.

To be sure, understanding the "Rules of Engagement" will enhance our witness as we reach out to those in our sphere of influence.

Again, evangelism is a process. Not only are we partnering with God in the Great Commission, we are also co-laboring in God's field. One sows, another waters, but God gives the increase (cf. 1 Corinthians 3:7).

Evangelism is a heart issue. As we surrender more of ourselves to the Lord in this area, the more ready we will be. We will see people more like the Lord does, and serve them more effectively as we share the gospel.

Evangelism is a Team Thing. As children of God, we're all part of the same team, the church. As we work together in fulfilling the Great Commission, have confidence that the Lord is bringing His game plan of redemption to fruition. Jesus said, "I will build My church and the gates of Hades shall not prevail against it" (Matthew 16:18).

So press on and be faithful in doing your part on the team—proclaiming the gospel boldly in word and deed—knowing that together we have the victory. "Now thanks be to God who always leads us in triumph in Christ, and through us diffuses the fragrance of His knowledge in every place" (2 Corinthians 2:14).

Chapter 1
Training Session

SPIRITUAL MUSCLE MEMORY

"And also if anyone competes in athletics, he is not crowned unless he competes according to the rules" (2 Timothy 2:5).

WARM UP

When you think of "engaging in evangelism," what thoughts, feelings, or images come to mind?

In your life what barriers have you faced in the area of personal evangelism?

PRACTICE DRILLS

Has your primary view of evangelism been that it's an event or process? What shaped that paradigm?

"Evangelism is discipleship and discipleship is evangelism." Agree or Disagree. Why?

Why is it important that our heart be aligned with God's heart in His passion for the lost?

What's your prevailing view of evangelism: "God does it all?" "I do it all?" or "It's a team thing?" What experiences have shaped that view?

As His witness, what does God require of us? As His witness what does God promise to us?

"One sows, one waters, but God gives the increase" (1 Corinthians 3:7). In your experience, how have you witnessed this principle play out in the evangelistic process?

MATCH TIME

Are you prepared to surrender more of your heart to the Lord in this area of personal evangelism? If yes, tell Him. If no, why not?

In what specific ways will your understanding of evangelism as a process alter your efforts to reach the lost?

In what specific ways will your understanding of evangelism as a team thing alter your efforts to reach the lost?

EXTRA TRAINING

Study Matthew 28:18-20, Matthew 9:35-39.

Chapter 2

Watching the Ball

For I delivered to you first of all that which I also received: that Christ died for our sins according to the Scriptures, and that He was buried, and that He rose again the third day according to the Scriptures.
1 Corinthians 15:3-4

Swiss Tennis Star Roger Federer is undoubtedly one of the best tennis players of all time. Some consider him the greatest. The French Open, Wimbledon Championship, the US Open, and Australian Open are the four most important annual tennis tournaments in the world, and are known as the "Grand Slams." As of this writing, Federer has won a record seventeen Grand Slam tournaments.

His grace, smoothness, and shot making ability are only matched by his class. Tennis is known as the gentlemen's sport and Federer is certainly that—a gentleman.

Amidst all of Federer's tennis exploits, one secret to his success might be overlooked by even the most ardent tennis observer: His laser-like vision.

Interestingly, he is cited as the perfect "ball watcher." His technique is legendary and key to his great success. In evangelism there is one essential component we must also keep our eye on. It is the main thing. If watching the ball is the main thing in tennis, then the main thing in our evangelistic efforts is understanding our message.

Our message is the gospel of Jesus Christ. The gospel is the main thing. As we seek to understand personal evangelism, keeping the main thing the main thing is imperative.

Cutting Through the Clutter

In the midst of the information age and advent of twenty-first century technology, we are bombarded with messages daily. It takes work to sift through the messages and determine what to ignore, what is important, and what to act upon. Yet, one message is singular, transcendent, powerful, and life changing. Amid the noise and clutter of a message-saturated world, it is simply the most important message of all.

What is that message? It is the gospel, the good news about Jesus. In fact, it is the very best news.

In 1 Corinthians 15:3-4, Paul articulates the gospel message: "For I delivered to you first of all, that which I also received, that Christ died for our sins according to the Scriptures, and that He was buried and that He rose again on the third day according to the Scriptures."

The gospel is about Jesus' life and what He accomplished on our behalf. Namely, He paid our sin debt, providing a means of forgiveness so that through faith in Him, we could be reconciled to God and receive the gift of abundant and eternal life.

The gospel message is as deep as it is wide. It is the topic of volumes and volumes of books. Yet for our purposes, I will touch on just some of the basics of our message. Writing a short chapter doesn't do it justice. The topic is that immense. We should continually study the profundity of the gospel and its eternal implications.

What the Gospel Is

While the central figure of the gospel is Jesus, the three main components of the gospel message are the Scriptures, substitutionary atonement, and the resurrection

First, the gospel message is based on the Scriptures. When Paul wrote his letter to the Corinthian church, "Scriptures" referred to the Hebrew Bible (the Old Testament). The letters comprising the New Testament had not yet been compiled into one volume. When we understand the Old Testament we will better understand the gospel as presented in the New Testament. It is good to understand how we got "here from there."

Jesus declared in Matthew 5:18 that He came not to "abolish the Law and the Prophets, but to fulfill." Talking with two men on the road to Emmaus (Luke 24:27), the Lord used the opportunity to teach. Luke records the event, "Beginning at Moses and all Prophets, He expounded to them in all the Scriptures the things concerning Himself." Just before His ascension, Jesus reiterated this truth to His disciples: "Thus it is written, and thus it was necessary for the Christ (Messiah) to suffer and rise from the dead on the third day" (Luke 24:44-46).

The New Testament makes the gospel clear, building upon the Old Testament. This understanding has helped my witness in sharing the good news about the Messiah with my Jewish people over the years.

Perhaps you've heard, "The Old Testament is the New Testament concealed and the New Testament is the Old Testament revealed." To fully understand the one it's imperative to study it in light of the other. The two testaments make up the whole counsel of God.

A second component of the gospel message is substitutionary atonement. This concept of substitutionary atonement is first illustrated for us in the Garden of Eden after the fall when God clothed Adam and Eve with tunics of skin made from a slain animal. Adam and Eve's covering of fig leaves was an unacceptable sin covering. Atonement must be found in God's provision rather than man's efforts. Substitutionary atonement, ancient Israel's means of forgiveness found throughout the Old Testament, is highlighted in Leviticus 17:11. "For the life of the flesh is in the blood, and I have given it to you upon the altar to make atonement for your souls; for it is the blood that makes atonement for the soul." Additionally, Isaiah

53 is a powerful messianic prophecy about the Suffering Servant's sacrifice on behalf of mankind:

> Surely He has borne our griefs
> And carried our sorrows;
> Yet we esteemed Him stricken,
> Smitten by God, and afflicted.
> But He was wounded for our transgressions,
> He was bruised for our iniquities;
> The chastisement for our peace was upon Him,
> And by His stripes we are healed.
> All we like sheep have gone astray;
> We have turned, every one to his own way;
> And the Lord has laid on Him the iniquity of us all.
>
> (Isaiah 53:4-6)

Substitutionary atonement finds its culmination in the person of Jesus, "The Lamb of God who takes away the sin of the world" (John 1:29). "For He made Him who knew no sin to be sin for us, that we might become the righteousness of God in Him" (2 Corinthians 5:21).

We study the New Testament to better understand what God has done for us in the person of Jesus Christ.

The third principle of the gospel, the resurrection, is essential to the message. This concept is found in various places in the Old Testament. For example, resurrection is referred to in Daniel 12:1-2:

> At that time Michael shall stand up,
> The great prince who stands watch over the sons of your people;
> And there shall be a time of trouble,
> Such as never was since there was a nation,
> Even to that time.
> And at that time your people shall be delivered, everyone who is found written in the book.
> And many of those who sleep in the dust of the earth shall awake, some to everlasting life, some to shame and everlasting contempt.

David expressed confidence in resurrection when he wrote, "For you will not leave my soul in Sheol, nor will you allow your Holy One to see corruption" (Psalm 16:10). Lastly, Job expressed confidence that he would see his Redeemer in physical resurrection in Job 19:25-27, when he wrote: "For I know that my Redeemer lives, and He shall stand at last on the earth; And after my skin is destroyed, this I know, that in my flesh I shall see God, Whom I shall see for myself, and when my eyes shall behold, and not another. How my heart yearns within me."

We typically think of resurrection as a New Testament topic, and it is. But we also see the concept expressed by Old Testament writers. Believers live in the light of the fulfillment of the future hope the biblical writers expressed. The empty tomb is our proof. We rejoice in that knowledge.

Jesus, in rising from the dead on the third day, demonstrated His authority and victory over sin and death. In fact, later in 1 Corinthians 15:17, Paul notes that, "If Christ is not risen, your faith is futile; you are still in your sins." Jesus resurrection was physical and literal. First Corinthians 15 is the most extensive chapter on the resurrection in the entire New Testament and is worth deeper study.

These three then—the Scriptures, substitutionary atonement, and the resurrection of Christ—comprise the gospel, whose singular figure is Jesus.

What the Gospel is Not

As Servants of the King, we need to know what our message is. And as we seek to be 'on point' about that message, knowing what our message is not will also benefit our witness.

First, the gospel is no bed of roses. We need to be careful about presenting the reality and cost of the gospel to a person. In fact, the cost of discipleship, the cost of following Jesus, can be great. Jesus said, "If anyone desires to come after Me, let him deny himself, and take up his cross daily, and follow Me" (Luke 9:23).

Jesus is not a panacea for all our ills, just the answer to our greatest need...the need for forgiveness. Jesus is not going to suddenly make everything in your life peachy. Believing in Jesus is no add on, no embellishment to our current life. I've many times in witnessing encounters shared with people that in many ways since I've trusted in Jesus, I experience many troubles and hardships because of my faith. But I add that my 'happiest day' apart from knowing Jesus pales in comparison to my "most difficult" day as a Christian. For I have love, joy, and peace that transcend my circumstances because of my relationship with God. Additionally, I have often said that I follow the truth (Jesus) regardless of the consequences, because it is the truth. God transformed my life, forgave my sins and has given me hope in today and a reason to get up tomorrow. And I have the promise of a glorious future—all this apart from my human circumstances.

Finally, the gospel is not our story. Although the gospel has touched our lives and changed the course of our story, our testimony is not the gospel message. My testimony is an intersecting of my story and His story and it is important to our witness—so much so, that we'll address it in a later chapter as we'll seek to better understand our narrative and articulate our testimony in everyday conversation.

Positive Implications of the Message

Believing in Jesus Christ brings a person into a right relationship with God. We are forgiven of and set free from the power of sin and death.

Jesus saves us from judgment and saves us to eternal life—"Most assuredly, I say to you, he who hears My word and believes in Him who sent Me has everlasting life, and shall not come into judgment, but has passed from death into life" (John 5:24).

Jesus came to give us life and give it more abundantly (John 10:10). He wants us to understand and know Him (Jeremiah 9:24).

Trusting in Christ means we have the Holy Spirit dwelling within us and as such are able to experience and express the 'fruit of the Spirit' found in Galatians 5:22—love, joy, peace, longsuffering, kindness, goodness, faithfulness, gentleness, and self-control. Who wouldn't want the blessings of these benefits?

And we could go on. Yet consider just some of the wonders of His Grace, the salvation He provides, and the future that awaits those who trust in Him:

Bless the Lord, O my soul, And forget not all His benefits: Who forgives all your iniquities, Who heals all your diseases, Who redeems your life from destruction, Who crowns you with loving-kindness and tender mercies, Who satisfies your mouth with good things, So that your youth is renewed like the eagle's. The Lord is merciful and gracious, slow to anger, and abounding in mercy. He will not always strive with us, nor will He keep His anger forever. He has not dealt with us according to our sins, nor punished us according to our iniquities. For as the heavens are high above the earth, So great is His mercy toward those who fear Him; As far as the east is from the west, So far has He removed our transgressions from us (Psalm 103:1–5; 8–12).

Blessed be the God and Father of our Lord Jesus Christ, who has blessed us with every spiritual blessing in the heavenly places in Christ, just as He chose us in Him before the foundation of the world, that we should be holy and without blame before Him in love, having predestined us to adoption as sons by Jesus Christ to Himself, according to the good pleasure of His will, to the praise of the glory of His grace, by which He made us accepted in the Beloved (Ephesians 1:3–6).

Blessed be he God and Father of our Lord Jesus Christ, who according to His abundant mercy has begotten us again to a living hope through the resurrection of Jesus Christ from the dead, to an inheritance incorruptible and undefiled and that does not fade away, reserved in heaven for you, who are kept by the power of God through faith for salvation ready to be revealed in the last time (1 Peter 1:3–5).

Painful Implications of the Message

Interestingly, there are painful consequences for believing in Jesus and painful consequences for rejecting Him. The painful consequences of believing in Jesus are exclusively in the temporal, for God has promised His children a sinless, perfect forever. In heaven "There will be no more death or mourning or crying or pain" (Revelation 21:4).

However, there is a cost associated with following Jesus in the here and now. If we want to fully identify with Him, then we're called to identify with Him in His suffering. He told His disciples: "A servant is not greater than his master. If the world hated Me, the world will hate you" (John 15:20).

No doubt, each believer has a cross to bear, and humanly speaking, it's not a warm fuzzy thing to experience and endure. Yet, this is the Jesus way. Yes, in the temporal, following Jesus is no bed of roses. Some of the negative consequences are rejection, misunderstanding, and conflict.

While a missionary in New York City I remember doing phone visits with a 20something Jewish man named Aaron, who lived in Philadelphia. His interest in speaking with me was to learn more about messianic prophecy. He was fascinated and thought the subject was "cool."

After a couple of Bible studies, I stopped him and said, "Aaron, let me tell you something. This is no fun and games. Do you understand the potential consequences of going down this path?" I told him about my coming to faith in Jesus and that because of my faith, my father and I had been estranged for many years. I let him know that if he continued down this road he might discover that Jesus is the Messiah and the fulfillment of these prophecies. I asked if he was prepared to deal with the consequences of what he might discover. If he came to realize Jesus is the Messiah, then would he believe in Him? I explained that if he did trust in Jesus as Messiah, he could lose his fiancée, his family, and his connection to the larger Jewish community.

I was compelled to share Jesus' words from Matthew 10:34–38 with him. "Do not think that I came to bring peace on earth. I did not come to bring peace but a sword. For I have come to set a man against his father, a daughter against her mother, and a daughter-in-law against her mother-in-law; and a man's enemies will be those of his own household. He who loves father or mother more than Me is not worthy of Me. And he who loves son or daughter more than Me is not worthy of Me. And he who does not take his cross and follow after Me is not worthy of Me."

That was the last Bible study we did over the phone, and that was okay. Aaron didn't call me again and didn't return my calls. Following the truth has consequences. I tell people that I follow the truth regardless of the consequences because *He* is the truth.

Temporal pain associated with following Jesus contrasts sharply with the eternal pain of rejecting Him.

In Luke 16, Jesus tells a sobering story of the rich man and Lazarus. He contrasts the experience of the rich man in Hades and the Lazarus in "Abraham's Bosom," an expression for heaven. Luke 16:19–31 is a vivid reminder of the eternal consequence of rejecting God's free gift of salvation. Paul made it clear: "For the wages of sin is death, but the free gift of God is eternal life in Christ Jesus our Lord" (Romans 6:23).

Jesus taught more about hell than any other person in the Bible. Hell is a reality perhaps not spoken of much in evangelism today, but it is a sobering aspect of the gospel message. When we are saved, we are saved from eternal separation from God.

God's desire is for everyone to be saved. He pleads with people to trust in Him. He "desires all men to be saved and to come to the knowledge of the truth" (1 Timothy 2:4), and he is "not willing that any should perish but that all should come to repentance" (2 Peter 3:9).

The Servant's Task

As servants in the King's court (our world), we need to be

stewards of the message entrusted to us, understanding it, and delivering it whenever possible.

When playing tennis you must carry a racquet. In the court of the King the imperative is that we carry the gospel message with us at all times.

For we are His ambassadors. And as such He's entrusted us with the good news. God is a God who wants His people to take His good news to those who've not yet heard. In Hebrew, *Besorah Tovah* means "glad tidings" or "good news." In the Old Testament, Isaiah wrote, "How beautiful are the feet of those who preach the gospel of peace, who bring glad tidings of good things" (Isaiah 52:7). The Greek word *evangelion* means good news or gospel. In Romans 11:14-15 the Apostle Paul articulates well our duty to proclaim the gospel to those who've not met the Savior: "How then shall they call on Him whom they have not believed? And how shall they believe in Him of whom they have not heard? And how shall they hear without a preacher? And how shall they preach unless they are sent?" The gospel is good news about Jesus. In fact, it's the very best news.

A Free Gift

As I mentioned in the preface, my father patterned a good work ethic for me to follow. I remember him saying, "Kid, there are no free lunches." It was his way of telling me that if I wanted something, I'd have to work to get it. In other words, I'd have to earn it.

The gospel message is a message whose central tenet is God's grace—Him giving us a salvation we don't deserve and can't earn.

This is one reason the Christian message is unique among all world religions. All other world religions are based upon the basic concept of "this do"; our Christian faith is based upon the reality of "this happened." All other world religions have some system of morals, codes of conduct, systems of behavior, when adhered to, allow the follower to go to heaven, nirvana, paradise, etc. The Christian faith is based upon Jesus' finished work on the cross. He did it all and that all is enough to save us from the penalty our sin deserves.

We are called to believe in Jesus in order to be saved. "For the wages of sin is death, but the free gift of God is eternal life in Christ Jesus our Lord" (Romans 6:23, NASB).

The concept of getting something for nothing is difficult for some to accept. By definition, all gifts are free to the recipient, but not to the giver. God paid a great price for the gift He offers us. The cost was Christ's death on the cross (John 3:16). The price Christ paid at Calvary is unfathomable. Yet this good news is God's means of forgiving us and making us His children.

God's grace is not cheap. It was very costly for Him. Yet, it's freely offered as a gift—something that can't be earned. It can only be received by faith.

A Warm Reception?

The good news about Jesus is based on the bad news about people. We're sinful and our sins have separated us from God. In fact, our sins made it necessary for Jesus to suffer unspeakable anguish and die. The bad news is also because of our sin the only thing we deserve from God is His eternal wrath and judgment. But God extended His mercy and grace in the person of Jesus, the Prince of Peace. And through faith in Him, we might have peace with God. That is the heart of the good news.

Yes, the Lord has made man in His image and He loves us with an everlasting love. Yes, we are of inestimable value. Yet, as image bearers we've been corrupted by sin and that sin separates us from a holy, perfect, and righteous God.

The gospel makes a statement about the inherent condition of man: we are not good. And this flies in the face of the common perception that man is inherently good. No, people are not good. Jesus Himself said that only God is good (Mark 10:18). We are sinful. David wrote, "Behold, I was brought forth in iniquity, and in sin my mother conceived me" (Psalm 51:5). In Jeremiah 17:9 the prophet stated, "The heart is deceitful above all things, and desperately wicked; Who can know it?"

We shouldn't be surprised that a message of the good news of God is couched in the bad news that something is terribly wrong with people. Naturally, we don't want to hear that we are born into and live in a state of depravity.

The late British journalist Malcolm Muggeridge put it this way: "The depravity of man is at once the most empirically verifiable reality but at the same time the most intellectually resisted fact."

Nobody likes to be the object of criticism, but the truth remains. What should we do with this uncomfortable knowledge about our spiritual condition? Pride will attempt to reject and rationalize it away. Humility will receive it and confess it before God. This blast of reality is not so quickly embraced. In the natural, no one is going to hear that message and respond, "Cool. I see your point. I'm a filthy, rotten sinner who needs saving." Such an admission is a supernatural work of the Holy Spirit showing us our sin and need for a Savior. He can move in the heart and bring us to a place where we can agree with God about our true condition. Then we can receive a new life through God's provision found in the person of the Lord Jesus Christ. For the Bible says, "Humble yourself in the sight of the Lord and He will lift you up" (James 4:10), and, "He who calls on the name of the Lord will be saved" (Romans 10:13).

We shouldn't harbor illusions about the nature of the message and people's response to it. Many will cringe and reject it; some will receive it and believe.

The gospel is polarizing. It creates a strong response when presented. Some will respond positively, others negatively, but there will be a response. Paul notes: "For the message of the cross is foolishness to those who are perishing, but to us who are being saved it is the power of God" (1 Corinthians 1:18). To illustrate, we need go no further than to examine the gospels and the book of Acts to see how people responded to Jesus and the Apostles as they proclaimed the gospel. It was always mixed.

As we serve in His court, we are called to be faithful to share this message. We can't control how anyone may respond. Remember, success in witnessing means to take the initiative to share the gospel in the power of the Holy Spirit, leaving the results to God.

A Picture of Faith

In John 3, Jesus presents God's plan of salvation to Nicodemus. Part of that dialogue includes this Old Testament reference: "And as Moses lifted up the serpent in the wilderness, even so must the Son of Man be lifted up, that whoever believes in Him should not perish but have eternal life" (John 3:14-15). Here the Lord refers to Numbers 21:4-9, where the Israelites are judged for their unbelief. God sent "fiery serpents among the people, and they bit the people; and many of the people of Israel died" (Numbers 21:6). When the Israelites confess their sin, they ask Moses to pray God would take away the serpents. After Moses prays, the Lord provides a lifesaving measure, "Make a fiery serpent, and set it on a pole; and it shall be that everyone who is bitten, when he looks at it, shall live." So Moses made a bronze serpent, and put it on a pole; and so it was, if a serpent had bitten anyone, when he looked at the bronze serpent, he lived" (Numbers 21:8-9).

A simple, yet profound act of faith was required in order to be healed from the deadly bite of the serpents. Those who believed and looked upon that serpent were saved from death. So Jesus used that event to make an analogy for Nicodemus and for us—that by looking upon Jesus and believing in Him, a person can be delivered from the wages of sin, death, and restored to a right relationship with God.

Who Saves Whom?

"For by grace you have been saved through faith, and that not of yourselves; it is the gift of God, not of works, lest anyone should boast" (Ephesians 2:8-9).

As servants in the Kings court, it's important to clarify and delineate between the roles and responsibilities of the servants and those of the King Himself. Regarding the message, our role is to proclaim the good news, but it is the Holy Spirit who enables people to understand and accept the message. Different roles. One desire:

that people would come to faith in Jesus.

God and God alone is the author of salvation. It is He who saves people and makes them His children.

On occasion, I've heard people share their witnessing frustration with a phrase like, "I just can't get so-and-so to see the light." As you've shared the gospel with people, you've probably experienced an individual who does not understand, or is confused by, or categorically rejects the message. My advice is, "Stop trying to get them to see the light. You can't. Only God can." Understanding the King is in control and the court is His domain, as is everything, will help us as His servants. While serving we're simply called to do our part, sow and water. It is God's part to give the increase. Servants do their part. The King does His part.

How a person responds to our message and what happens in their heart is between them and God. There are spiritual dynamics at work that are unique to the gospel message and recipients of that message.

The gospel is based on spiritual wisdom, not human wisdom. First Corinthians 2:13-14 states: "These things [divine wisdom] we also speak, not in words which man's wisdom teaches but which the Holy Spirit teaches, comparing spiritual things with spiritual. But the natural man does not receive the things of the Spirit of God, for they are foolishness to him; nor can he know them, because they are spiritually discerned." (See also 1 Corinthians 1:18-2:16).

God needs to supernaturally reveal the truth to people: "No one can come to Me unless the Father who sent Me draws him; and I will raise him up at the last day" (John 6:44). See also John 6:65. It is the work of God, not ours, that opens the eyes of the blind.

At this point it would be appropriate to acknowledge the tension between man's free will and God's sovereignty. It's clear that Scripture teaches that men and women are free moral agents: "For whoever calls on the name of the Lord will be saved" (Romans 10:13.)

It is also clear that God is sovereign in salvation, meaning it is He who saves people according to His will. So how is it that when we reject His offer of salvation, we are responsible and when He saves us, it is His sovereign grace? How do we reconcile this paradox? We don't. God tells us in Isaiah 55:8-9, "My ways are higher than your ways and My thoughts higher than your thoughts." As God's children we simply need to acknowledge that our Father in heaven knows best. And as His children we're called to take God at His word and walk by faith. As my pastor says on occasion, "One of the first things we'll say when we get to heaven is, 'Of course.'"

Regardless of what you believe about this aspect of salvation, it's immaterial to the church's effort to fulfill its role in the Great Commission. God commands us go out and make disciples of all nations, for His invitation for reconciliation with sinners is universal. "For God so loved the world that He gave His only begotten Son, that whosoever believes in Him should not perish but have everlasting life" (John 3:16). We are called to sow gospel seed, to be His witnesses, and live as salt and light in a lost and dying world.

We can't save anyone from their sins. People don't save themselves from their sins. God's gift of salvation is received by faith and faith alone. "For by grace you have been saved through faith, and that not of yourselves: it is the gift of God, not of works, lest anyone should boast" (Ephesians 2:8-9).

So don't try to get them to see the light. As you witness, ask the Lord to open up spiritual eyes so they may see, understand and accept the truth, then believe in Jesus.

In tennis, keeping the eye on the ball is imperative, even for the accomplished tennis player. Like Roger Federer's laser-like vision on the ball, we should have laser-like vision on our message.

We need to keep the main thing—the gospel—the main thing. When we do, we will stay on point. Without the gospel message, what is it we proclaim? Without the gospel message, what can we truly offer people?

We are ambassadors for Christ. "We have been approved by God to be entrusted with the gospel" (1 Thessalonians 2:4). Therefore, understand the message, continue to study the message, thank and praise God for the message, share the message, and trust that our Father in heaven will use the message to accomplish His perfect will.

"Sing to the LORD, bless His name. Proclaim the good news of

His salvation from day to day" (Psalm 96:2).

Chapter 2
Training Session

SPIRITUAL MUSCLE MEMORY

"For I delivered to you first of all that which I also received: that Christ died for our sins according to the Scriptures, and that He was buried, and that He rose again the third day according to the Scriptures" (1 Corinthians 15:3-4).

WARM UP

Why is it important to be clear and confident about the gospel message?

PRACTICE DRILLS

What do you think most surprises people about the gospel message itself?

What was your initial response to the gospel? How have you seen others react to the gospel?

What are your thoughts and feelings about there being negative implications of the gospel, both for the believer and unbeliever?

What did you learn from this chapter to help people "get it?"

MATCH TIME

Write out your own understanding of the gospel based upon what you've learned in this chapter.

How will a deeper understanding of the gospel message affect your own witness to others?

EXTRA TRAINING

Study 2 Corinthians 5:17-21.

Chapter 3

The Opposition

*For we do not wrestle with flesh and blood, but against principalities,
against powers, against the rulers of the darkness of this age, against
spiritual hosts of wickedness in the heavenly places.*
Ephesians 6:12

The 2010 Wimbledon Tennis Championship was the occasion for
the longest match in tennis history. In the Men's Singles
tournament first round, the twenty-third seeded American John Isner
defeated French qualifier Nicolas Mahut after eleven hours, five
minutes of play spread over three days. The final score of 6-4, 3-6, 6-
7, 7-6, 70-68 comprised a total of 183 games. It was a battle many
called the "endless match," setting all-time records both by time and
number of games played.

I remember it well. I was in Asheville, North Carolina with my
wife Lori. As we stepped into a local restaurant, I noticed the match
on television. When I saw they were well into the fifth set, I was
astonished. I tried to explain what was happening to Lori. We finished
our meal and left. The match continued on.

The opposition was not only the player on the other side of the
net, but also the competitor's own body, a body that was being tested
to the limits of human endurance. This tennis match was truly a mind-
blowing physiological challenge. Dehydration and muscle fatigue
could defeat either competitor. A tennis match that typically goes
more than three hours is considered a long match. This one lasted

more than eleven hours over three days.

One sports surgeon said the players had risked dehydration, hyperthermia, and kidney damage, and that one or both might suffer "some sort of injury or persistent problem over the next six months: shoulder problems, tendonitis, and recurrent knee problems."

The men faced a twofold opposition: the competitor on the other side of the net and their own failing bodies.

I witnessed many hard fought matches in my years as a college tennis coach. Two competitors, bashing shot after shot over the net, each point hotly contested. Hours later, after lots of sweat, emotion, and a handful of game-changing points, the match concluded—one player victorious, the other gallant in defeat. We called a match like that a *war*. The Isner-Mahut match was one such war.

In the spiritual realm, especially in the arena of personal evangelism, you and I are in a war too. This is not a metaphor. This is for real. Yet it's not the kind of war that results in temporary glory or defeat. Rather, you and I are smack dab in the middle of a spiritual conflict where the eternal state of the souls of men and women hang in the balance. Sound serious? It is.

We are also soldiers in the army of the Lord. Being a soldier implies there is the potential for active combat. In the Kingdom of God, we as His servants are in a constant state of war whether we realize it or not. The combat is not optional. There is a war going on in the court of the King.

Part of the spiritual war takes place on the battlefield of personal evangelism, and if the opposition can't keep us from witnessing, then they will simply attempt to make our witness as weak as possible.

So evangelism is difficult because there are forces working against us. Those forces fighting against our personal witness include not only outside opposition, but opposition from inside us.

The Opposition Inside

The opposition within us, is characterized in the Scriptures as the "old man," "the flesh," or our "sinful nature." In short, it's our selfishness, rather than Christ's righteousness, that at any particular moment, dominates us. And when we walk according to our flesh, it's not good.

The Apostle Paul wrote these words about the debilitating effects of the flesh: "For I know that in me (that is, in my flesh) nothing good dwells; for to will is present with me, but how to perform what is good I do not find. For the good that I will to do, I do not do; but the evil I will not to do, that I practice" (Romans 7:18-19).

When operating according to our flesh, we become experts at rationalizing away the need for evangelism.

John Starke notes in a *Gospel Coalition* blog entitled "Why Don't I Evangelize?" — "There are lots of ways to justify not practicing evangelism: I don't have the gift of evangelism. I'm not very persuasive. I'm too shy. There are lots of unspoken reasons as well. I suppose the most common is fear."

Sometimes we give up before we even start because we say it's too hard. Let's bring this one home. In my flesh I could say these things about engaging the personal evangelistic process: "I can't do it." "I don't know what to do." "I won't know what to say." "It's too risky." "I can't handle rejection." "I don't like the person." "I don't want to deal with it. It's too messy and too much work."

Do you relate to any of those?

What's a poor soul to do? Is there something that can overcome those destructive salvos of discouragement and defeat? Yes, it is to walk in the Spirit.

"I say then: walk in the Spirit, and you shall not fulfill the lust of the flesh. For the flesh lusts against the spirit and the spirit against the flesh; and these are contrary to one another, so that you do not do the things that you wish" (Galatians 5:16-17).

When we walk in the Spirit, we have the power to do God's will, including the service of evangelism. Yes, "I can do all things through Christ, who strengthens me" (Philippians 4:13), and so can you. "And God is able to make all grace abound toward you, that you, always having all sufficiency in all things, may have an abundance for every good work" (2 Corinthians 9:8). So do we really have any good excuse to not engage in evangelism? No.

The Opposition Outside

The war waged against us from the outside emanates from the devil and his minions. As Bible teacher John McArthur has said "When you declare allegiance to heaven, you declare war on hell. And hell fights back pretty hard."

1 Peter 5:8 states, "Be sober, be vigilant; because your adversary the devil walks about like a roaring lion, seeking whom he may devour." He's talking about you and me. "For we do not wrestle against flesh and blood, but against the rulers of the darkness of this age, against spiritual hosts of wickedness in the heavenly places" (Ephesians 6:12). The enemy of our souls would do anything and everything within his power to keep us from sharing the life-giving message of the gospel.

Tennis is called a gentleman's game, but make no mistake, in the game of life Satan is anything but a gentleman. He plays for keeps. He hates God's children to the core, and his desire is to thwart any and every attempt to share the gospel with anyone at any time. Not only does he want to defeat us, he would destroy us if he could.

The devil's strategy of opposing our Christian life is referred to by the Apostle Paul in Ephesians 6:11 as "wiles of the devil." In our evangelistic efforts, he seeks to render us less effective in these ways:

Condemnation. Satan condemned Job before God (Job 1:9-11), accused believers before God in heaven (Revelation 12:10), and plants condemning thoughts in our minds about our weaknesses to do the work of evangelism. He'll plant thoughts like these in our minds:

"You can't do it."

"You don't know what you're talking about."

"They won't listen."

Any of those thoughts ever run through your head? Unlike tennis, this is no gentlemen's game. This is warfare.

Distraction. Satan loves for us to fall into temptation. Temptation keeps us from doing God's will. He is called the "god of this age" (2

Corinthians 4:4) and the "ruler of this world" (John 16:11). He constantly allures us with temporal things that distract us from eternal things. Paul exhorted believers in Colossae: "Set your minds on things above, not on things on the earth" (Colossians 3:2).

Regarding your spiritual life, which includes evangelism, do you ever feel distracted by earthly things? We all do at times.

The biblical concept of "world" in one sense is the evil system under Satan's spell. Specifically, it's the system of belief, attitudes, and actions that opposes the things of God. In our effort to witness to others, the "world" is against God and hence against us sharing the good news of Jesus. As believer's we're called to categorically reject its sway. "Do not love the world or the things in the world. If anyone loves the world, the love of the Father is not in him. For all that is in the world—the lust of the flesh, the lust of the eyes and the pride of life—is not of the Father but is of the world. And the world is passing away, and the lust of it, but he who does the will of God abides forever" (1 John 2:15-17).

In this Age of Tolerance and Relativism, it's not politically correct to proclaim absolute truth and declare Jesus the only way to heaven. The hard truth is this: world system opposes the things of God. For example, the world says we should, "Look out for No. 1," while Jesus teaches us to love our enemies, serve others, and give our lives away. My father used to echo a common worldly theme, "Larry, the meek shall not inherit the earth." In contrast, Jesus said in Matthew 5:5, "Blessed are the meek, for they shall inherit the earth."

The world system that opposes our Christian witness says, "How arrogant, bigoted, and narrow-minded of you to say there's only one way to heaven. Absolute truth—come on. Jesus, God in the flesh? Who are you kidding?"

There are real spiritual reasons that may cause us to avoid personal evangelism. If you've been one to shy away or shudder when confronted with the need to engage the process, take heart. There are real reasons you have been hesitant. We noted earlier, but it bears repeating: When we declared allegiance to heaven by trusting in Jesus we concurrently declared war on hell and hell fights back pretty hard.

Yes, there are weapons leveled against us, but God has also equipped us with armor and a sword with which to fight the good fight of faith:

> Finally, my brethren, be strong in the Lord and in the power of His might. Put on the whole armor of God, that you may be able to stand against the wiles of the devil. For we do not wrestle against flesh and blood, but against principalities, against powers, against the rulers of the darkness of this age, against spiritual hosts of wickedness in the heavenly places. Therefore take up the whole armor of God, that you may be able to withstand in the evil day, and having done all, to stand. Stand therefore, having girded your waist with truth, having put on the breastplate of righteousness, and having shod your feet with the preparation of the gospel of peace; above all, taking the shield of faith with which you will be able to quench all the fiery darts of the wicked one. And take the helmet of salvation, and the sword of the Spirit, which is the word of God; praying always with all prayer and supplication in the Spirit, being watchful to this end with all perseverance and supplication for all the saints (Ephesians 6:10–18).

Satan and His Scorched Earth Strategy

If it weren't enough that the devil opposes our evangelistic efforts at every turn, he also exerts much effort in opposing the hearing, understanding, and reception of the gospel message among people who've not yet met Christ. In short, he not only opposes we who seek to share, but also those who need to hear.

The persons we seek to reach are in spiritual bondage and our task is to proclaim the message of liberation and freedom found in the person of Jesus Christ. In the midst of this battle, Satan has several strategies for keeping unbelievers blind to the truth. Chuck Lawless puts it well:

"The enemy provides the lies to which unbelievers cling, such as 'I'm good enough,' and 'I can always wait until tomorrow to follow

God.' He makes sin attractive and alluring, convincing the unbeliever that following God will mean a loss of pleasure. He snatches away the Word of God before it takes root in an unbelievers heart (see Matthew 13:3-9, 18-23). More specifically, Satan blinds unbelievers to the gospel by promoting distorted views of the gospel itself."

I met Chet while serving as the outreach pastor of my church in East Tennessee. He was a parent I had met while doing ministry at a local school and we struck up a friendship. Knowing I was a Christian, Chet was curious about Jesus and the Bible. We began meeting regularly at a coffee shop for Bible study.

Chet was not a Christian. He said he was a Wiccan, but was open to learning about Jesus and the Bible. We did a few Bible studies. I shared the gospel mostly from the gospel of John, but along the way felt I needed to share a bit from Ephesians 6, a chapter dealing with spiritual war. I wanted to share the reality of spiritual warfare, not from a believer's point of view, but from a different bent. I talked about the fact that he would be getting thoughts in his head that would say, "Larry's an idiot and Jesus and the Bible are pipe dreams." I was simply warning him. I wouldn't say sharing Ephesians 6 with him is standard operating procedure, as witnessing conversations can go in numerous directions, but since he was dabbling in the spiritual, I wanted to apprise him of the spiritual war he was in. I encouraged him to seek God, asking Him to confirm the veracity of the claims of Jesus, the Bible, and the gospel.

In the parable of the soils we read about seed that lands on shallow ground and how it is snatched away. After a few Bible study sessions Chet seemed to be tracking well and understanding the gospel message. We made plans for the next study and as usual we'd confirm via phone.

The next time I tried to contact him, I only got an answering machine. Then after leaving several messages over the next few weeks, his phone was disconnected. I never saw Chet again.

You could say that he may have moved, or had a crisis that precipitated the phone being turned off. But there is no denying he wanted no contact with me. I believe there was a spiritual war component to this series of events.

We Are Victorious

God has given us victory over our opposition. Jesus said on the cross, "It is finished" (John 19:30). In His death and resurrection He defeated sin and death. Our Lord also said, "I will build My Church and the gates of Hades shall not prevail against it" (Matthew 16:18). So let us walk in the manner in which we've been called—victory. Consider the following:

Our flesh. "Walk in the Spirit, and you shall not fulfill the lust of the flesh" (Galatians 5:16).

The devil. "He [God] who is in you is greater than he [the devil] who is in the world" (1 John 4:4).

The world. "For whatever is born of God overcomes the world. And this is the victory that has overcome the world—our faith" (1 John 5:5).

In the next chapter we'll explore other divine resources God has given us as we strive to fulfill the Great Commission.

We need to be realistic about this victory God has accomplished and the opportunity for us to walk in that victory. The paradox is that while the victory has been accomplished and the outcome undeniably determined, there are skirmishes still taking place, battles still raging on the court, and we know that very well.

But never forget that we, as His Church, know how the story ends. We've read the book. We win! The rub is that the enemy of our souls, Satan, and his minions, who know the outcome is already determined, continue to fight the battle anyway.

In May of 1999, I was completing a seventeen month ministry tour with The Liberated Wailing Wall, the mobile evangelistic music team of Jews for Jesus (I sing and play guitar.) After serving fifteen months on the mainland of America and Canada, we were sent on a two-month world tour. We concluded our tour stopping in Hawaii on our way back to California. We spent about a week doing church presentations and "suffering for Jesus" on the beautiful island of

Oahu.

One day my teammate Thane and I toured Pearl Harbor. It was a moving experience as we took a boat ride to the USS *Arizona* Memorial. Standing atop the sunken battleship, oil from the ship still rising to the surface, was humbling beyond words. We were standing where World War II began for the USA on December 7, 1941. Also humbling was gazing across the harbor and seeing the USS *Missouri*—the ship upon which the Japanese officially surrendered on September 2, 1945. We were standing where the war began and gazing at the ship where the war officially ended.

I've pondered that day in light of Christ's redemptive work. We all will one day experience the ultimate cessation of hostilities on God's very own USS *Missouri*: the eternal city called New Jerusalem and Heaven. The victory is certain.

At the end of the war, Japan's government was charged upon their official surrender to enforce the cessation of hostilities. But there were instances in the vast Pacific theater where a lag time existed—time elapsed before some Japanese and American soldiers warring on isolated islands "received the memo" and ended their hostilities. Additionally, there were some Japanese soldiers who didn't believe the news that the war had ceased and continued to fight. While the war was declared over, some Japanese soldiers continued fighting for a time.

We walk in victory and we as His servants are on the way to the *Missouri*—that being heaven. In the interim, we serve in His court—this world. But our enemy, Satan and his minions, continue hostilities in spite of the fact that Jesus won the war when He defeated sin and death at His death and resurrection. In this war the defeated army has not surrendered. We take on the defeated foes of the King doing His bidding. We do so understanding the victory is certain; the war already won. Though we will get battered and bloodied, it's worth it, for we know we'll ultimately experience that time of rest.

Revelation 21:4 tells us that in glory, "God will wipe away every tear from their eyes; there shall be no more death, nor sorrow, nor crying. There shall be no more pain, for the former things have passed away."

So in the present we're called to serve the King by getting into the water and playing our part in helping save those who are drowning. God has so many more that He will be rescuing from death and will bring to safety. We can praise and thank God that He's given us an opportunity to play a role.

Just as the Lord called Peter to get out of the boat and into the water in Matthew 14:29, so He calls us to get out of the boat and enter the fray. People are drowning and need to be rescued. In the mystery of the gospel, He uses people like you and me to save them.

Some of us think we're terrible swimmers, some even try to say they can't swim. Others are afraid of sharks, of drowning themselves, or of some other negative circumstance—real or imagined. Yet He's calling us.

Yes, we're in a spiritual war and our testimony to people about God's grace found in Jesus Christ is one of the battlefields. But the next time you feel like giving in to those forces working against you and not engaging in this area of personal evangelism, remember God has won the war, victory is certain, and in the mystery of the Kingdom He wants us to be faithful as we fight the good fight of faith.

"Thanks be to God, who gives us the victory through our Lord Jesus Christ" (1 Corinthians 15:57).

Chapter 3
Training Session

SPIRITUAL MUSCLE MEMORY

"For we do not wrestle with flesh and blood, but against principalities, against powers, against the rulers of the darkness of this age, against spiritual hosts of wickedness in the heavenly places" (Ephesians 6:12).

WARM UP

Why is it important to understand the opposition as we engage evangelism?

PRACTICE DRILLS

What are specific examples of reasons you either don't engage or feel inadequate about engaging the evangelistic process?

What struck you most about those forces that stand in opposition to your witness? Discuss.

How have you experienced opposition to your witness? How have you sought to overcome it?

MATCH TIME

Identify what you think is your stiffest opposition to engaging in the evangelistic process and how you will now stand against it.

EXTRA TRAINING

Study Romans 7:13-25; 1 Peter 5:8-11: 2 Corinthians 4:1-6

Chapter 4

Our Equipment

For though we walk in the flesh, we do not war according to the flesh.
For the weapons of our warfare are not carnal but mighty in God for
pulling down strongholds, casting down arguments and every high
thing that exalts itself against the knowledge of God...
2 Corinthians 10:3-5

Until the 1960s, rackets were made of laminated wood. American tennis star Jimmy Connors was at the fore of the tennis racquet revolution in the 1960s when he debuted the "Wilson T2000,"—a steel racquet. The T2000 set wood racquet traditionalists on their ears with its lightweight steel construction. It didn't warp, provided ample power and its slender framework meant less wind resistance.

Jimmy Connors wasn't just a tennis professional using cutting edge technology as a stunt. He was one of the greats of his time. From 1974 to 1977 he held the top world ranking among professional tennis players for a then-record 160 consecutive weeks. He held a year-end top ten world ranking for a record setting sixteen years. Growing up, Connors was one of my favorite players.

Connors' popularization of the T2000 led to a racquet revolution in the 70s and 80s, as the modern game transitioned from the standard wooden tennis racquet to racquets made of graphite and other lightweight composite material.

Growing up in the 1970s, I learned how to play with the old

wooden racquet and then transitioned into composites as a teenager. One of the advantages of the T2000 and other metal racquets was that if thrown, they would only bounce and bend. The wood racquet would easily crack and could break. As a youth using a wood racquet helped me control my temper after missing a shot. Throwing the wood racquet was not a good option. After a bad shot what's a frustrated boy to do? I learned the hard way not to throw the "stick." Today, the wood racquet is obsolete—well not completely. In our son Elijah's room we have an old wooden racquet attached to one of his walls as a decorative piece.

Although today's tennis racquets have been caught up in the technology revolution they are still tennis racquets.

The tennis racquet is SOE: standard operating equipment. And there are a couple of other items on the tennis SOE short list: tennis balls, tennis shoes, and proper attire. Without these you can't play the game.

When it comes to the evangelistic endeavor, we also have an SOE short list. This spiritual equipment is necessary for properly engaging in a personal witness.

In evangelism our SOE includes the Word, The Gospel, The Spirit, and Prayer.

We had our rivals in the Southern Conference. To prepare for a big tennis match, we'd practice, talk about what we needed to do to put ourselves in position to win, both individually and collectively. We made sure we were prepared and understood what it was going to take to be successful. We knew we could be in for a long afternoon of tennis. Sometimes these affairs lasted as long as five hours. We needed to be prepared.

In addition to our SOE, each of our players would have several extra racquets. As a team we had lots of liquids, a first aid kit in case someone got injured, a trainer on hand, energy bars, bananas, and more. Competitive tennis matches can be quite involved. It takes a well-coordinated operation to play a college tennis match.

In our chapter on "The Opposition," we noted that there are spiritual forces opposing our witness. That's why engaging in personal evangelism is such a battle. As in a tennis match we will utilize the appropriate equipment in the battle, so our weapons in the spiritual warfare involving evangelism need to be at hand, ready to use.

In early September 2004, I was in Colorado for a couple of weeks helping lead an evangelistic campaign with Jews for Jesus. One night during one of our witnessing "sorties," I led a group of six people to the Pearl Street Mall, a four block pedestrian mall in Boulder, Colorado. The pedestrian area stretches from 11th Street to 15th Street along Pearl Street and is home to a number of businesses and restaurants as well as the Boulder County Courthouse.

As you may know, Colorado is a bastion for New Age and occult activity. As was normal protocol, just before our team began handing out literature and talking to people about Jesus, we would say a prayer. You know, "Lord, open up doors and hearts...Amen." After a brief prayer, we dispersed and went on our mission. Ninety minutes later we met to debrief what God had done. Everyone was discouraged because we got stonewalled—in a spiritual sense. People were not open and we didn't have many meaningful gospel conversations. Each of us shared a similar experience.

I understood one thing. The next time we come to this place, it would be different. I told the leader of our campaign to send me back to the Pearl Street Mall, for I wanted to try another strategy. A few days later I took another group there.

This time I gave our group specific instructions. Since we're in a spiritual war, one of the weapons of warfare at our hand is prayer. Before we prayed I paired our group into 2 person teams. I assigned one team to prayer walk for twenty minutes. I told them not to engage anyone and not to hand out any literature. Simply pray over the locale, for the people, for our witness and for the Lord to move. Every twenty minutes another two-person team would take over. For the entire ninety minute mission we had a prayer team lifting up the effort and imploring the Lord to work.

What do you imagine happened? Doors opened and God moved. It so happens that we all experienced much more freedom in sharing, more open hearts, more evangelistic literature distributed, and more and deeper witnessing conversations.

This was a tremendous object lesson for me in understanding the power of prayer in evangelism. It's one thing to understand and use the equipment so to speak. It's another to access with greater commitment those resources the Lord has given us.

That was street evangelism, I know. Yet the principle applies in our typical course of activities where we're seeking to share the gospel with people in our own sphere of influence.

I share this story to highlight our spiritual battle and the necessity of utilizing the divine resources (our spiritual SOE) God has given us.

Remember, "We are not sufficient of ourselves, rather our sufficiency comes from God, who has made us sufficient as ministers of the new covenant" (2 Corinthians 3:5-6).

One of the reasons we are sufficient for all the things He's called us to—including the work of personal evangelism—is that "God is able to make all grace abound toward you, that you, always having all sufficiency in all things, may have an abundance for every good work" (2 Corinthians 9:8). Yes, in His Grace He has made us sufficient and in His Grace we are able to engage all He calls us to.

There is no way to overestimate the power of these resources as we seek to reach the lost. Certainly books are written on each of these resources and the great impact they can have on our witness. For our purposes, we're touching upon them.

God's Word

The Bible is the infallible, inspired, inerrant word of God. It is wholly trustworthy and accurate. It's God's love letter to man and blueprint for reality. I like Alvin Reid's comments: "The Bible gives us objective verifiable information about God and our relationship to Him. However, it is fundamentally a book of faith. The Bible does not tell us everything we want to know about reality, but it does tell us everything we need to know."

Romans 10:17 states: "Faith comes by hearing and hearing by the Word of God." This is true for both the Christian and for the one who hasn't yet met Christ.

In Ephesians 6, the Apostle Paul describes the spiritual war that the devil and his minions wage against us. In verses 10-18, Paul describes the whole armor of God we are to put on in this fight. In verse 17, he notes the only offensive component of the armor: the "Sword of the Spirit," the Word of God.

In our day of media abundance and technological tools, how we share can be varied: Facebook and other social media, email, books, tracts, personal notes, through audio and video recordings and links. In addition to these means of communicating God's Word, we can also share His Word in a traditional fashion, reading the Bible person to person. There is no end to the available delivery systems. The goal is to share the Word of God and let it do what it does—accomplish His will.

Let's return to the Parable of the Sower:

> Behold, a sower went out to sow. And as he sowed, some seed fell by the wayside; and the birds came and devoured them. Some fell on stony places, where they did not have much earth; and they immediately sprang up because they had no depth of earth. But when the sun was up they were scorched, and because they had no root they withered away. And some fell among thorns, and the thorns sprang up and choked them. But others fell on good ground and yielded a crop: some a hundredfold, some sixty, some thirty. He who has ears to hear, let him hear. (Matthew 13:3-9)

The Parable Explained

Therefore hear the parable of the sower: When anyone hears the word of the kingdom, and does not understand it, then the wicked one comes and snatches away what was sown in his heart. This is he who received seed by the wayside. But he who received the seed on stony places, this is he who hears the word and immediately receives it with joy; yet he has no root in himself, but endures only for a while. For when tribulation or persecution arises because of the word, immediately he stumbles. Now he who received seed among the thorns is he who hears the word, and the cares of this world and the deceitfulness of riches choke the word, and he becomes unfruitful. But he who received seed on the good ground is he who hears the word and understands it, who indeed bears fruit and produces: some a hundredfold, some sixty, some thirty. (Matthew 13:18-23)

Whatever methodologies and strategies we employ, at the end of the day, we must share God's Word with the people we're seeking to reach. God tells us in Isaiah 55:10-11: "For as the rain comes down, and the snow from heaven, and do not return there, but water the earth, and make it bring forth and bud, that it may give seed to the sower and bread to the eater, so shall My word be that goes forth from My mouth; It shall not return to Me void, but it shall accomplish what I please, and it shall prosper in the thing for which I sent it."

Jesus said in John 8:32, "You shall know the truth and the truth shall set you free." The truth of God's word is a most powerful weapon.

Andrei Sakharov was a Russian nuclear physicist, anti-Soviet dissident and human rights activist. He became renowned as the designer of the Soviet Union's "Third Idea," a codename for Soviet development of thermonuclear weapons. Sakharov was an advocate of civil liberties and civil reforms in the Soviet Union. He was awarded the Nobel Peace Prize in 1975.

Late in his life, the man who gave the Soviet Union the bomb stated, "The most powerful weapon in the world is the truth."

Sow the seed of truth, God's Word, the most powerful weapon in the world, entrusting the results to God. For only He truly knows the condition of the soil and only He is the source of increase.

The Gospel

Yes, I know—we spent an entire chapter on the Gospel. But

remember, there are three keys to learning: repetition, repetition, and repetition.

We focused earlier on the 3 major components of the gospel: the Scriptures, Substitutionary Atonement, and Resurrection. Now I'd like us to touch upon the person who embodies the gospel itself—Jesus.

Alvin Reid notes, "The gospel is not so much an idea or a thing as it is the announcement of a person. We believe Jesus Christ is the embodiment of the good news from God to man."

Mark 1:1 starts his gospel account with, "The beginning of the gospel of Jesus Christ." New Testament writers in several places refer to *proclaiming* or *preaching* Jesus. For example, the Apostle Paul wrote "we proclaim Him" (Colossians 1:28) to the church in Colossae and in Galatians 1:16 he mentions his calling to "preach Him among the Gentiles."

The gospel is all about Jesus. Why? Because:

First, Jesus is God (John 1:1, Titus 2:13-14).

Second, Jesus lived, died on the cross for our sins, rose again from the dead and ascended into heaven (1 Corinthians 15:1-5).

Third, Jesus is the only way to a relationship with God. He said, "I am the way, the truth, and the life. No one comes to the Father except through Me" (John 14:6).

Finally, "Salvation is found in no one else. For there is no other name under heaven given among men by which we must be saved" (Acts 4:12 NASB)

In God's Word we find the message that saves—the gospel message that is the person of Jesus, who He is and what He has done for us. In the midst of an ocean of messages, this one message is singular, transcendent, powerful, and life changing. It is simply the most important message of all.

The Holy Spirit

Personal evangelism is done in and through the power of God—at least evangelism that is fruitful and glorifies God. In the book of Zechariah, Zerubbabel was encouraged to complete the Temple rebuilding project after the Lord brought the Jewish people back to Jerusalem in 538 BC. God spoke about this effort by saying it would be completed, "'Not by might nor by power, but by My Spirit,' Says the Lord of Hosts" (Zechariah 4:6).

More directly, Jesus in John 15:5, says, "Without me you can do nothing." When applied to evangelism, our personal witness needs to be both Spirit-led and Spirit-empowered.

"Evangelism without the Holy Spirit is like a body without a soul," D. Miles said.

God the Holy Spirit indwells each believer. He is the one who empowers us to witness. Just before the risen Jesus ascended into heaven, He gave this promise to the disciples in Acts 1:8, "You shall receive power when the Holy Spirit has come upon you; and you shall be witnesses to Me in Jerusalem, and in all Judea and Samaria, and to the end of the earth."

The Holy Spirit helps us know what to say. In Luke 12:12 we see Jesus teaching the disciples to not fret about what they might say when undergoing persecution, telling them, "The Holy Spirit will teach you in that very hour what you ought to say." While in our witnessing efforts we do want to strive to always be ready to share when God provides opportunities, we need to also trust in the power of the Spirit to know when and what to share.

Additionally, the Holy Spirit gives us boldness. In Acts 4 after Peter and John had healed a lame man, they were arrested and forbidden by the Sanhedrin to speak or teach in the name of Jesus. Upon their release they went and prayed with other believers, asking God to give them boldness to speak His word. "And when they had prayed, the place where they were assembled together was shaken; and they were all filled with the Holy Spirit, and they spoke the word of God with boldness" (Acts 4:31).

I desperately need the Holy Spirit in my personal witness to others. I need Him to fill me, to empower me, to help me know what to say, and to give me courage. How about you?

Prayer

In competitive tennis, the one constant for every player is a need to develop a baseline level of fitness. In tennis you have to move. Before you can hit the ball you first have to *get* to the ball. This requires an adequate fitness level. Additionally, one must develop an adequate degree of endurance. If you tire quickly, then your effectiveness can be greatly compromised. This concept of baseline fitness is true for many sports. Coaches and athletes will tell you that no matter your skill level, if you haven't attained a minimum level of physical fitness, then you're defeated before you even enter the arena, field, or court.

Even if you're a recreational player, you need a baseline fitness level. You have to be able to walk and move. You can't have injuries like a shoulder or arm problem that would preclude you from swinging the racquet. We all understand that.

Fitness is crucial, regardless of the level of tennis you're engaged in. With that said, even fit athletes aren't guaranteed positive results. Fitness simply allows you to enter the fray.

To have any degree of effectiveness, any opportunity to bear fruit in the King's court, we must understand that prayer is our baseline for spiritual fitness. Prayer acknowledges our dependence upon the Lord to guide us, to move in the hearts of those we desire to reach, and to work in and through the circumstances of life wherever the evangelistic process occurs.

We need to bathe everything in prayer, including our evangelistic effort. In 1 Thessalonians 5:17, the apostle wrote: "Pray without ceasing." Of what was he speaking? Perhaps the ambiguity speaks of an overarching theme to always be in a spirit of prayer.

I would recommend a great website filled with biblical prayers called kingdompraying.com. Dr. Kevin Meador has done a great service for the church in providing prayers for various areas, including prayers for the lost, prayers for open doors, and more. Using Bible verses for prayer is powerful and fruitful.

Prayer is one piece of our spiritual equipment that makes Satan shudder. Prayer is a must if we wish to have any success when we enter the arena. Ralph Herring states: "That Satan trembles when he sees the weakest saint upon his knees, why not make him tremble? Why not storm the very gates of hell? Nothing could please God more. In the conflict that is upon us, certainly we can ill afford to neglect one weapon Satan does not have in his arsenal and the one he fears most—prayer."

Now that's putting fear into your opponent.

We've touched upon the why of prayer. Now let's talk about what to pray for (based on 1 Peter 3:15):

A Right Heart. "But in your hearts sanctify Christ as Lord." Give him more of your heart in this area, a heart that breaks for the lost.

Readiness. "Always be ready to give an account." Prepare to share.

A Right Spirit. "With gentleness and respect." Our witness should be a humble witness.

In addition, we should also pray for:

Peace. "Be anxious for nothing, but in everything by prayer and supplication with thanksgiving, let your requests be made known to God and the peace of God, which surpasses understanding, will guard your hearts and minds through Christ Jesus" (Philippians 4:6-7).

Wisdom. "Walk in wisdom toward those who are outside, redeeming the time" (Colossians 4:5).

Open Doors. "Continue earnestly in prayer...praying also for us, that God would open to us a door for the word, to speak the mystery of Christ" (Colossians 4:2-3). Ask God to give you opportunities to share the gospel with others.

The Lost. "The Lord opened her [Lydia's] heart to heed the things spoken by Paul" (Acts 16:15). Ask God to move in the heart of those who need Him, that they would be open to hear, that they would be enabled to understand the gospel, to the end that they would believe in Jesus.

Other Witnesses. "Then He said to His disciples, 'The harvest is plentiful, but the laborers are few. Therefore pray the Lord of the harvest to send out laborers into His harvest" (Matthew 9:35). Since evangelism is a team effort, pray God would send other believers to be salt and light to others, even among those with whom you have a direct witness.

Divine Appointments. Finally, I encourage you to pray for divine appointments. These open doors to share the gospel are orchestrated by the Holy Spirit and can include many of the prayer specifics we've mentioned above.

I teach a six hour seminar called the PEP Course—a personal evangelism primer. One of our participants named Peggy, after attending the seminar, shared a powerful testimony of what God did after she prayed a simple prayer of faith one day. Her story illustrates much of what we've been discussing in this book:

Peggy woke up one Sunday morning and for the very first time asked the Lord for a divine appointment. She and her traveling group were going to do some farm tours in Western North Carolina that day. She says the group she traveled with somehow ended up at a farm they had not intended to see. Along the tour, the guide, a young man in his twenties, stopped during a break and shared some of his personal struggles. The farm served as a rehabilitation facility for those experiencing addiction issues, and Peggy noted that the man spoke of trusting in a "higher power" in his battle with addiction. As she listened to the young man share, she took the initiative to specifically ask him what he thought about Jesus. This opened up the conversation that culminated a few minutes later when someone in her group led this young man in a sinner's prayer to receive Christ. Peggy added his countenance was immediately different as he shared how he felt his burdens were lifted. Praise God.

What a wonderful testimony of God working mightily through her simple prayer.

This divine resource called prayer, along with the Word of God, the Gospel, and the Holy Spirit, comprise our equipment to do the work of evangelism.

As we engage in the evangelistic endeavor as servants in His Court, may we depend on these essential divine resources, "our equipment," in order to do the work He's called us to.

So onward Christian soldier. By faith access and appropriate these divinely bestowed resources and walk in the manner in which you've been called—in victory: "For whatever is born of God overcomes the world. And this is the victory that has overcome the world—our faith" (1 John 5:5).

Chapter 4
Training Session

SPIRITUAL MUSCLE MEMORY

"For though we walk in the flesh, we do not war according to the flesh. For the weapons of our warfare are not carnal but mighty in God for pulling down strongholds, casting down arguments and every high thing that exalts itself against the knowledge of God...." (2 Corinthians 10:3-5)

WARM UP

What will happen in our evangelistic efforts if we don't understand or if we neglect our divine resources?

PRACTICE DRILLS

What have been some of your experiences in utilizing the "equipment" in your witness?

How has the use of any of our divine resources equipped your witness?

What piece of spiritual "equipment" are you most reliant on and what resource are you least reliant on in your personal witness? Why do you think that is?

What have you learned about utilizing the noted spiritual "equipment" discussed in the chapter?

How can prayer change your personal witness in light of the material discussed?

MATCH TIME

How will you practically utilize these divine resources in your own personal witness?

Consider memorizing a key passage or passages as part of an ongoing evangelistic training program.

EXTRA TRAINING

Study Ephesians 6:10-18; Isaiah 55:10-11.

Chapter 5

A Well-Balanced Game

And heal the sick there, and say to them,
"The Kingdom of God is at hand."
Luke 10:9

Andre Agassi would win eight Grand Slam titles, but when he began the 1992 Wimbledon Championship, the 22 year-old had not won any. With a No. 14 world ranking at the time and the knowledge that grass was Agassi's worst surface, few figured the 1992 event at the All England club would produce his first major title.

Professional tennis matches have much to do with a player's style of play and the surface of the court. Grass courts are more suited to those with big serves. Grass courts also favored those who could back up the serve with a good volley, a shot taken out of the air closer to the net. Andre Agassi's strength was not his serve, but rather his return of serve. And he wasn't much of a volleyer. His strength was hitting balls from the back of the court, the baseline. He did not play a grass court warmup event before Wimbledon, where he was seeded 12th. Agassi's unlikely path to victory began to take shape as he pulled off a shocker in the quarterfinals when he knocked off No. 4 seeded Boris Becker, a three-time Wimbledon champion who had reached the final six of the previous seven years.

Agassi then beat two more serve-and-volley masters in the semifinals and final, knocking off John McEnroe and Goran

Ivanisevic respectively to take the title at age twenty-two.

Andre Agassi turned the service return into a devastating offensive shot. So much so that he won the most famous tennis tournament in the world—Wimbledon—not with the serve, but with the service return.

Andre Agassi would prove himself capable of winning tennis matches on all playing surfaces as he is one of the few players to have completed a career grand slam—winning all four major tennis tournaments in his career: Wimbledon (grass courts), the French Open (clay courts), the Australian Open (hard courts) and US Open (hard courts).

Each playing surface demands unique skill sets and abilities. Accomplishing the career grand slam is a testament to the complete game Andre Agassi possessed. He was very accomplished both at playing offensive tennis and playing defensive tennis.

It takes both a good offensive and good defensive game to be an overall good tennis player.

Being strong in one area and weak in the other won't take a player very far in competitive tennis. One must be able to retrieve shots and simply keep the ball in play, and at the same time, when opportunity arises, one must be able to be aggressive and hit a winning shot.

These are the two basic pillars in tennis and in many other sports—offense and defense.

In personal evangelism there are two pillars that compose a well-rounded witness: demonstration and proclamation—show and tell.

Show and Tell

There's a reason we used to do show-and-tell in school. One without the other is incomplete, the audience will be left wanting, and we'll be scratching our heads wondering why they didn't quite understand.

Biblical evangelism is about showing and telling the gospel. It's not an either/or proposition. And when we do it well, we'll make the greatest impact for Jesus.

I should clarify that people can't know Christ without the

proclamation of the gospel. As we've noted: "faith comes by hearing and hearing by the Word of God" (Romans 10:17). People can come to Christ without a visible demonstration of good news and in some settings do. I've led people to the Lord on many occasions through simply sharing God's plan of salvation in word and people responding in faith. While good deeds can get people's attention like few words can, good deeds alone will not lead a person to faith in Christ. So it's important to not mistake good deeds for good news.

In our context of personal relationships, especially those where we have regular touch points with an individual, we're simply talking about this general principle of show and tell. For we should be sensitive not only to people's spiritual need for Jesus, but also to physical needs that can provide opportunities to show His love.

Good Deeds and Good News: Jesus' Ministry

Jesus' ministry was characterized by both good deeds and good news. He was and is the epitome of a witness for God, which we might expect since He is God's Son.

The Apostle Peter summarized Jesus' ministry in Acts 10:36-38: "You know the message God sent to the people of Israel, telling the good news of peace through Jesus Christ, who is Lord of all...[and] how God anointed Jesus of Nazareth with the Holy Spirit and power, and how He went around doing good."

After feeding the 5000, Jesus said to them, "I am the Bread of Life. He who comes to Me shall never hunger and he who believes in Me shall never thirst" (John 6:35).

Interestingly, Jesus' good deeds weren't bestowed upon people because of their worthiness, but because of their need. Just before feeding the 4000 in Matthew 15:32, Jesus said to his disciples, "I have compassion on the multitude because they have now continued with Me three days and have nothing to eat. And I do not want to send them away hungry, lest they faint on the way."

In sum, Jesus ministry was characterized by good deeds and good words.

Pillar #1: Good Deeds

As witnesses for Jesus, we can recognize and meet needs in order to demonstrate the love of God. In our sphere of influence, looking for ways to serve people and meet needs can be a wonderful initial engagement in the evangelistic process.

What that may look like for you is unique to your sphere of influence. What can you do? What needs do you see? With whom do you start? Well, how about with one person. We can't serve everybody, but we can serve somebody.

Reaching out to one person can make a huge difference. You may have heard the story of the boy walking along the beach with his father. A recent storm had washed thousands of starfish onto the beach, and many of them were dying. The boy began stooping over and tossing the starfish back into the surf. The puzzled father asked, "With thousands of dying starfish stranded here on the beach, what difference do you think you can make?" Without breaking stride, the young boy picked up another starfish, lobbed it into the sea, then said, "Well, Dad, I just made a difference for that one."

As we've mentioned, on a person's journey to faith, they typically will have many touch points with the gospel. Good deeds play a part in that journey.

Let's not have any illusions about attempting to sow gospel seeds into people's lives through service. Understand that there are people who won't respond the way we'd like or aren't interested in us meeting needs they may have. In Luke 17:11-17, Jesus heals ten lepers, yet only one returned to Jesus, giving thanks and glorifying God. Jesus, in His omniscience, knew only one would return, yet it didn't prevent him from healing them all nonetheless. Jesus healed them not because they would respond, but because they were broken and had a need.

Eric Swanson and Rick Rusaw in their book *The Externally Focused Quest*, provide excellent perspective regarding good deeds and their place in our evangelistic efforts: "Although we believe there is no more fertile ground for evangelism than selfless service, we serve not to convert but because we have been converted. We serve not to make others Christians but because we are Christians. People are worthy recipients whether they become Christ followers or not. Evangelism is our ultimate motive, but can never be our ulterior motive for serving."

John Stott, regarding our motives in doing good deeds, adds, "To sum up, we are sent into the world, like Jesus, to serve. For this is the natural expression of our love for our neighbors. We love. We go. We serve. And in this we have (or should have) no ulterior motive. True, the gospel lacks visibility if we merely preach it, and lacks credibility if we who preach it are interested in only souls and have no concern about the welfare of people's bodies, situations and communities. Yet the reason for our acceptance of social responsibility is not primarily in order to give the gospel either a visibility or a credibility it would otherwise lack, but rather simple uncomplicated compassion. Love has no need to justify itself. It merely expresses itself in service wherever it sees need."

With this healthy perspective in mind, we need to always be ready, expecting God to open doors so we can share His love in word and deed. Swanson and Rusaw state, "Good deeds create goodwill, and goodwill is a wonderful platform for good conversations about the good news."

When we serve people with no strings attached, we can also pray expectantly for God to move those we serve with curiosity about why we're doing what we're doing. So when people in our sphere of influence experience our good deeds, we need to be ready to answer the question: "Why are you doing this?"

Born (Again) to Serve

"For we are His workmanship, created in Christ Jesus for good works, which God prepared beforehand that we should walk in them" (Ephesians 2:10).

Jesus said about Himself, "For even the Son of Man did not come to serve, but to serve and to give His life a ransom for many" (Mark 10:45). As servants of Jesus, we are also called to serve and to give our lives away.

Our witness should be characterized by service. And how do we serve those we desire to reach? We can serve them by praying for them and by looking for opportunities to demonstrate God's love in tangible ways. We're familiar with the expression, "People don't care how much you know until they know how much you care." That pithy little catchphrase packs a punch. The potential impact of our service to others is great.

While we may be given group opportunities to serve as part of a local church family or with a service organization like a food pantry or mission, acts of service for people in our personal sphere of influence require us to be more intentional and relational.

A few years ago, I attended an Outreach Conference for Churches just outside of Atlanta at a church that was making a fantastic contribution to the life of their community.

One of the leaders from that host church noted his church's outreach to the community was very simple—it just required lots of "want to" and lots of "elbow grease." It's that simple. All it took was intentionality, effort, and follow-through.

Many of the challenges associated with the evangelistic process tend to be weighted on the side of gospel proclamation rather than demonstration. And that's what most of this book focuses on. Yet, there is a real challenge in demonstration, and that is the sacrifice of service. For serving others requires time and relational investment, both of which we are hard-pressed to give up. Yet people are of such great value to the Lord that we must make the effort to serve others.

While serving as the local outreach pastor of my home church in Johnson City, TN, sacrificial service was central to our outreach strategy. Our leadership sought to encourage our church family to get involved and get "our hands messy." As we grew in our sacrificial service, so our church's impact grew in our community.

Aside from the "want to," service also required a "meet the need" mentality. Our church asked, "What needs do we see and how can we serve to best meet those needs in our community?" Our mantra was: "Under promise and over deliver." If we say we'll do something for someone, then do it and do it well. Because to promise to do something and not do it harms our testimony and our credibility.

In your sphere of influence, what needs are before you? Is there someone in your life who needs transportation to run errands? Perhaps there are house projects you could do, or lawns you could cut. If a neighbor is ill, you could bring them a home-cooked meal. If you're good with cars, you could offer to change their oil. Whatever your gifts and abilities, the willingness to give them away in Jesus' name is a wonderful testimony. Offering to lend a hand if there is a need is a great way to get involved in someone's life. There are many ways to individually serve people in your sphere of influence.

Be Ready for the "Why?"

While serving others in Jesus' name we need to be prepared for the "Why?" When the recipient asks, "Why are you doing this?" we must be ready with an answer.

Our answer goes like this: "Because I am a follower of Jesus and I want to follow His example of love through service to others." The Lord will give you the right words at the right time. Ask Him to prepare you with an answer to "Why?"

The wonderful thing about serving the people in our lives is that there will be many more opportunities to serve them as a continuing witness.

And the end game?

"Let your light so shine among men that they may see your good works and glorify your father who is in Heaven" (Matthew 5:16).

The demonstration of the gospel puts hands and feet to our faith and demonstrates how seriously we take the teachings of Jesus. For our theology should become biology.

In a world where "looking out for #1" is the norm, "looking out for our neighbor" is a distinctive the Lord can and will use to impact others.

So, be intentional, be available, and be relational, looking to glorify the Lord, testifying of His love through service to your neighbor. And whether a person is drawn closer to Jesus as a result, keep loving them, keep praying for them, and keep serving them unconditionally. This causes our servant's heart to grow and gives Jesus glory.

Pillar #2—Good News

While we want to be the hands and feet of Jesus, we also need to remember that "Faith comes by hearing and hearing by the Word of God" (Romans 10:17).

We've already discussed the message of the gospel at length. But I want us to think a moment about the newsworthiness of the gospel and its associated ramifications.

The Kingdom of God, when compared to the Kingdom of this World, is what some call the "Upside-Down Kingdom." We see the Upside-Down Kingdom introduced by Jesus in His Sermon on the Mount:

"Blessed are the poor in spirit, for theirs is the kingdom of heaven. Blessed are those who mourn for they shall be comforted. Blessed are the meek, for they shall inherit the earth" (Matthew 5:3-5). And that's only the beginning.

"You have heard that it was said, 'An eye for an eye and a tooth for a tooth.' But I tell you not to resist an evil person. But whoever slaps you on your right cheek, turn the other to him also. If anyone wants to sue you and take away your tunic, let him have your cloak also. And whoever compels you to go one mile, go with him two. Give to him who asks you, and from him who wants to borrow from you do not turn away. You have heard that it was said, 'You shall love your neighbor and hate your enemy.' But I say to you, love your enemies, bless those who curse you, do good to those who hate you, and pray for those who spitefully use you and persecute you" (Matthew 5:38-44).

The world says, "Look out for No. 1. Get all the gusto you can. Live for the moment. The strong shall inherit the earth. Love your enemies? Do good to those who hate you? Turn the other cheek? Get real, man."

You get the idea.

Talk about counterculture. The gospel is counter to our culture and therefore truly newsworthy, but it's not the kind of news coming out of major news outlets. It's not only good news, it's the very best news. And it's the news others need to hear and understand.

My very first job was delivering an afternoon paper. I was a twelve year-old delivery boy. While I was concerned about doing a good job delivering the news, the content of that news was unimportant to me. As believers, the content of the news we deliver is of utmost importance.

In one sense you might say we as believers are *newsmakers* when we demonstrate the gospel and *news reporters* when we proclaim the gospel message. The Apostle Paul himself said about the gospel: "For I delivered to you first of all that which I also received: that Christ died for our sins according to the Scriptures, and that He was buried, and that He rose again on the third day according to the Scriptures" (1 Corinthians 15:3-4).

When Jesus sent out the disciples for the first time in Luke 10, His commission included both demonstration and proclamation. He commanded them to "Heal the sick there, and say to them, 'The kingdom of God has come near to you'" (v. 9).

As fluid and organic as personal relationships are, neither proclamation nor demonstration will take the lead. Allow God in His providence to work that out.

We simply need to be ready when He opens those doors.

The important thing is that over time in our personal relationships, our personal witness will be most complete when it includes both the demonstration and proclamation of the gospel.

Truth Without Love

Proclamation without demonstration lacks authentication. It is truth without love. If I tell you about God's love found in Christ and then fail to show that love, then my testimony is weak and you may think me a hypocrite. Believers are often accused of being hypocrites and of pounding others with our view of righteousness. Being an effective witness for Jesus means I must back up my proclamation of truth with the demonstration of truth. If God is love and it is He I proclaim, then I need to take the initiative to authenticate the claims of the Savior by loving others in deed.

In the game of tennis, "love" means nothing—no points or games. But in the game of life it means much. It's one thing to proclaim truth; it's another to love those with whom you're sharing it. This is unconditional love: "Love suffers long and is kind; love does not envy; love does not parade itself, is not puffed up; does not behave rudely, does not seek its own, is not provoked, thinks no evil; does not rejoice in iniquity, but rejoices in the truth; bears all things, believes all things, hopes all things, endures all things" (1 Corinthians 13:4-7).

Love Without Truth

Demonstration without proclamation lacks explanation. It is love without truth. Some people think we can love people into the kingdom just by doing good works. If those you serve don't hear why you do what you do, then they'll be in the dark regarding your motivation. Worse, they'll be in the dark about the gospel message itself. There are many humanitarian institutions doing great work serving humankind, but their goal is not the salvation of others.

Christians do good works to glorify the Lord, not to glorify themselves. For example, people help others across busy streets all the time. One person, who thinks he or she is a good person, may help an elderly person across the street because it's not only a good thing to do, but it makes them look good. The person doing this good deed may not know Christ. In fact, there are many people who do great works in the name of humanity, compassion, self-glory, or because it's just the right thing to do. On the other hand, Jesus came not to be served but to serve others. He is our example. This is why we love in deed. At the end of the day, it's about Jesus' glory, not ours. It has always been about glorifying God. If a person is starving and I give him physical bread today, yet he dies tomorrow without hearing about the Bread of Life, then what have I given him?

Additionally, without an explanation, people on their own may come to erroneous conclusions by just observing the work of God. In Acts 2:12-13, when the Holy Spirit fell upon the believers at Pentecost, onlookers were "amazed and perplexed, saying to one another, 'Whatever could this mean?' Others mocking said, 'They are full of new wine.'" The people needed God's Word to explain the *why* of what they saw. Peter stands up and says, "Let this be known to you and heed my words..." He goes on to share from the prophet Joel about the coming of the Holy Spirit and then shares the gospel message. God used Peter's explanation to bring 3000 souls into the Kingdom of God (Acts 2:41).

Good deeds may authenticate the good news, but we must communicate the good news to explain the meaning of our good deeds.

A Complete Lesson

As a tennis coach, I've worked with every level of player, from world-ranked touring professionals to raw beginners. And one constant of the coaching process is to show and tell. It's one thing to tell someone how to hit a tennis ball. But people understand and learn best when I've shown them the technique. It's one thing to tell a student, "This is how it works." It's another thing to tell them and then show them how it works. And though that takes more effort, ultimately it will be the most effective means of communication.

We learn more through audio/visual presentations. Just as lessons are clearer and more powerful when heard and seen, so it is with the gospel. When it's displayed powerfully and proclaimed with clarity it will have the greatest impact. Tennis lesson anyone?

One Last Shot

Proclaiming and demonstrating the gospel helps communicate and authenticate the message. When we seek to be salt and light in our world, keeping these two pillars in perspective will help shape our gospel testimony. Each of us is inclined to lean one way or the other. But a powerful testimony is a both/and proposition.

Some say people would rather see a sermon than hear one, but perhaps the most compelling sermon of all is the visual sermonic—a beautiful and powerful combination of the love of God demonstrated and proclaimed.

Where do you lean? Is God wanting you to grow in one area or another? How can you practically apply what He's showing you in your daily life? These are good questions to take before the Lord as we seek to be witnesses for Jesus He desires us to be.

So go out in the power of the Holy Spirit and show and tell of God's great love and good news found in Jesus—to the Glory of God and for the building of His Kingdom.

Chapter 5
Training Session

SPIRITUAL MUSCLE MEMORY
"And heal the sick there, and say to them, 'The Kingdom of God is at hand.'" — Jesus (Luke 10:9)

WARM UP
In your personal witness, what comes easier—demonstration or proclamation? Why?

PRACTICE DRILLS
When you think of personal evangelism, do you more naturally move toward proclamation or demonstration? What in your life has shaped that leaning?

What gifts and abilities do you possess that you can use to demonstrate God's love in your sphere of influence? With whom can you share these gifts and abilities?

What will need to happen for you to serve people unconditionally—with no strings attached—knowing they might not respond positively or be open to hearing about Jesus?

MATCH TIME
Ask God to reveal the pillar He wants you to grow in (proclamation or demonstration) and determine what next steps you will take.

EXTRA TRAINING
Study John 6:1-40.

Chapter 6

The Game Plan

And He said to them, "Why do you seek Me? Did you not know that I must be about My Father's business?"
Luke 2:49

Manuel Orantes was known as Manuelito, "Little Manuel." Big Manuel was Manuel Santana, a hero for a previous generation of Spanish tennis fans. Santana was a four time major champion in the 1960s. Manuel Orantes was a humble man and didn't mind being "Little Manuel." Yet in epic fashion this modest man was elevated to tennis fame through an ingenious game plan he executed to perfection to win the biggest match of his career.

Orantes won his only major championship, the 1975 US Open, by defeating world No. 1 ranked Jimmy Connors in shockingly easy fashion: 6-4, 6-3, 6-3.

One sports writer echoed the sentiment of many tennis experts and fans alike after Orantes' U.S. Open triumph when he wrote that "almost nobody gave him a prayer against Connors."

How did Orantes do it? It was his game plan going into the match. He knew he couldn't defeat the hard-hitting Connors by trying to match him shot for shot. Instead, he played counterpuncher. He used a biting backhand slice to pull the defending champion to the net and then hit passing shot after passing shot to win points. Orantes also kept the ball low and short to Connor's forehand groundstroke with the same backhand slice, never allowing Connors to get in rhythm and causing many forehand errors.

If you play tennis, you get this. If you've never picked up a racquet, this may sound like Greek to you...and you don't speak Greek.

Pardon the pun, but the point is that having a game plan made all the difference for Orantes and, in our evangelism endeavors, having a game plan also makes a positive difference.

Orantes had a plan he executed in the big match. He planned for success and executed his plan leading to a glorious victory. You and I also can think about our life and witness in terms of executing a game plan—God's plan.

Jesus certainly had a game plan for life.

In thinking about life and our evangelistic endeavors we also need a plan of engagement. Jesus' life was completely centered around a plan: God's plan of redemption.

When Jesus was just a boy of twelve years He was separated from His family while in Jerusalem for Passover. His relieved parents found Him in the Temple, talking with the religious leaders. Upon finding Him, Mary said to Jesus, "Why have you done this to us? Look, Your father and I have sought You anxiously." Jesus responded in Luke 2:49, "Why did you seek Me? Did you not know that I must be about My Father's business?"

Jesus had a game plan: to be about the Father's business. As His servants we have been given a game plan: "For we are His workmanship, created in Christ Jesus for good works, which God prepared beforehand that we should walk in them" (Ephesians 2:10).

C.S. Lewis felt this way about the Father's business. "The glory of God, and, as our only means of glorifying Him, the salvation of souls, is the real business of life."

In the area of personal evangelism, our agenda is to follow Jesus, being His witnesses in word and deed and pointing people to Him. Jesus said, "Follow me and I will make you fishers of men" (Matthew 4:18-20). He also says, "Go and make disciples of all nations...and I will be with you always" (Matthew 28:19-20). He reiterates the agenda in Acts 1:8, "But you shall receive power when the Holy Spirit has come upon you; and you shall be witnesses to Me in Jerusalem, and in all Judea and Samaria, and to the end of the earth." Jesus' agenda was to be about the Father's business and that should be our agenda.

Intentionality in Reaching Out

An important component of the Father's business is intentionality—an intentionality that reaches out to the least and the lost. In this, as in all things, Jesus is our example.

In John 4, Jesus speaks with the Samaritan woman at a well. Notice His intentionality in verses 3 and 4: "He left Judea and departed again to Galilee. But He needed to go through Samaria." The backstory to this account is important. Jews and Samaritans harbored a hatred for each other that went back hundreds of years. Jews considered Samaritans "half-breeds" due to the intermarriage that occurred when the Northern Kingdom of Israel was exiled to Assyria seven centuries earlier. Jewish people traveling this route usually avoided Samaria, choosing to go around it rather than step on Samaritan soil. Yet we read Jesus "needed to go through Samaria."

In Jesus' day it was culturally taboo for a Jewish man to talk with a woman in public. Jesus not only talks with a woman, but He speaks to a *Samaritan* woman. And not any Samaritan woman, but a Samaritan woman who had five husbands in the past and was now with another man. This woman was considered an outcast among her own people. The Lord had to go through Samaria to minister to an outcast of the outcasts and share "living water" with her, revealing His identity as Messiah.

Another example of Jesus' being intentional in His outreach is found in Luke 19:1-10. Here the Lord, as He's passing through a crowd at Jericho, calls to a rich tax collector named Zacchaeus, who is sitting in a tree: "Zacchaeus, make haste and come down, for today I must stay at your house" (Luke 19:5).

As a tax collector for Rome, Zacchaeus was also an outcast, despised among his own Jewish people. The crowd took exception, saying in Luke 19:7—"He [Jesus] has gone to be a guest with a man who is a sinner." We can only imagine their dismay at Jesus' choice of a dinner host.

After Zacchaeus turned to the Lord, Jesus said, "Today salvation has come to this house, because he also is a son of Abraham; for the Son of Man has come to seek and to save that which was lost" (Luke 19:9-10).

The Lord taught several parables illustrating the agenda of passionately pursuing the lost. In Luke 15, Jesus taught the parables of the lost sheep, lost coin, and lost son. And what was the pursuit characterized by? Love. Love expressed in word and deed.

In 1987 I was coaching at a tennis academy in Largo, Florida. I was twenty-three years-old, just a year out of college. In December, I became a believer in Jesus and everything about my life changed—including my reason for living.

Before I came to believe in Jesus I had no real game plan in my life—you might say I was wingin' it. I really didn't know who I was and I certainly didn't know where I was going, both in the immediate as a tennis coach and in the eternal after I died.

Yet a decision to trust in Messiah Jesus changed that. All of a sudden, the tennis court was no longer simply about helping people improve their tennis game. It also became a platform to share the Father's love. My game plan for coaching came to be about not only the academy's business but ultimately about my Father's business.

As God opened doors, I would share my faith with those in our tennis academy. In fact, the first person I ever led to Christ was a guy who was training at our academy and needed a place to bunk for a couple of days before heading home. That was a great blessing.

Among my friends I shared how my life had been transformed—that I who previously was empty and without hope, now had joy, peace, purpose, and most importantly, forgiveness for my sin.

Now it's not as if my unbelieving friends said, "Larry, that's great man. Where do I sign up for this deal?" Rather, after a while, they didn't want to hear the "Jesus freak" tell them what a difference the Lord had made in my life.

In the evangelistic game plan God's given us, within the context of our lives, God wants us to be about His business. That business includes intentionality in reaching out to others with the hope they would come to know Christ.

Regardless of whether a person comes to know Christ, we as God's ambassadors of reconciliation are to love them, serve them, and pray for them. This ought to be an intentional and constant component of our testimony as we seek to be about our Father's business in the game plan of life.

Pointing People to Jesus

Jesus' earthly agenda included pointing people to Himself as the Messiah and Savior. This is well illustrated in Luke 4:16-21:

So He came to Nazareth, where He had been brought up. And as His custom was, He went into the synagogue on the Sabbath day, and stood up to read. And He was handed the book of the prophet Isaiah. And when He had opened the book, He found the place where it was written:

"The Spirit of the Lord is upon Me,

Because He has anointed Me

To preach the gospel to the poor;

He has sent Me to heal the brokenhearted,

To proclaim liberty to the captives

And recovery of sight to the blind,

To set at liberty those who are oppressed;

To proclaim the acceptable year of the Lord."

Then He closed the book, and gave it back to the attendant and sat down. And the eyes of all who were in the synagogue were fixed on Him. And He began to say to them, "Today this Scripture is fulfilled in your hearing."

Not only did Jesus point to Himself (see also John 3:16, John 5:24, Luke 4:16-21) others specifically pointed to Jesus for salvation:

- The Father pointed people to Jesus for salvation (Matthew 4:16-17).
- The Holy Spirit pointed people to Jesus for salvation (John 15:26).
- John the Baptist pointed people to Jesus for salvation (John 1:29).
- The New Testament saints pointed people to Jesus for salvation (John 15:27, the Book of Acts).

Ambassadors for Christ

In 2 Corinthians 5, the Apostle Paul reminded the believers in Corinth that they were "Ambassadors for Christ" and as such were given the Ministry of Reconciliation. What is an ambassador? In the time of Christ it described a man who served as a representative of a king from one country to another. In this passage, Paul describes this role for all believers as representatives of the King of Heaven, Jesus.

As His ambassadors, our agenda ought to be directly tied to God's agenda. Paul continues in 2 Corinthians 5:20, "Now then, we are ambassadors for Christ, as though God were pleading through us: we implore you on Christ's behalf, be reconciled to God."

Reconciliation is about the *lost* being *found.* "For God so loved the world that He gave His only begotten Son, that whoever believes in Him should not perish but have everlasting life" (John 3:16). In our sphere of influence we know people or have met people whose response to this concept of lostness is, "I'm not lost. I'm good." That's okay. It doesn't change our agenda to love them, pray for them, serve them, and hope that sometime soon they will recognize their need—their need to be found.

Where is Your Samaria? Who is your Zacchaeus?

As we've noted, a big part of God's agenda is to seek out and save the lost. We ought to be about our Father's business. Where is He working in your sphere of influence? Know that God is working in the hearts of men and woman all around us all the time. We need to understand this by faith and continue to point people to Jesus.

How passionately are we pursuing the least and lost, in word and deed pointing them to Jesus for salvation? Where is your Samaria? Who is your Zacchaeus? Is God wanting you to go somewhere and/or reach out to someone in your sphere of influence, someone in need of Jesus?

Chad and Angelia's Story

Chad and Angela attend my home church and share about their Samaria and their Zacchaeus:

We were both very satisfied in our professional lives, our kids seemed happy, we'd just bought a new house, and we even belonged to a great church. It was looking like the plans we'd made for our lives were well on their way to being fulfilled. As a teacher and a social worker we even felt like we were helping people. In spite of us having a good and happy life, we began to ask the question, God, is this it?

It took around five years to fully unpack, but we both knew that God didn't send Jesus Christ to walk among men so we could simply study the word and worship his Holy name. We knew that he wanted to live in and through us. Our family verse during this time was Hebrews 11:1, 'Now faith is confidence in what we hope for and assurance about what we do not see.' The plans we'd made for our future were beginning to change.

On April 15, 2012 we saw a need in our church bulletin for a family to serve as missionaries in Tarakan, Indonesia. Despite the fact that we'd never even discussed being missionaries, we left that day knowing that our lives were about to change. By July 8, 2012, we had resigned from our jobs, sold our house, and left our plans behind to be missionaries on a small island in Indonesia.

Although we went to serve "officially" as educators for missionary kids, we knew our family was called to do so much more. Living in a Muslim country, not speaking the language, learning how to eat the food, adjusting to the hot, tropical weather, and literally being brought to our knees...what could we do? Simple, love others as Christ loves us.

One of our most powerful experiences in love was an amazing relationship we were able to build with a young boy we affectionately referred to as Little Buddy. When we first arrived in Tarakan we began to see this boy all over town, and quickly realized that he was watching us with a deep curiosity. Little did he know that we were watching him too. As we began to interact with him we couldn't help but feel like our language skills might keep us from saying the right thing. Well, it didn't take us long to realize that this wouldn't be a problem. Not because our mastery of the Indonesian language grew by leaps and bounds, but instead because we quickly realized that he was deaf. Despite the verbal communication barrier, God's love brought us together.

In the beginning of our friendship, Little Buddy's smile was small and others watched our interactions with great curiosity. Through looks and sometimes even words we were asked, "Why are you hanging out with him, and why are you allowing him to sit at your table?" Over a transformational period of ten months we witnessed God's plan—Little Buddy's smile was bright and beautiful. But the most amazing thing was that others began accepting him and were open to our friendship.

We are not sure if our little buddy knew we were believers but, he knew we were with a missions organization. The locals also connected us as Westerners with that mission. During this wonderful season we witnessed God's plan in one sense was bringing people together, no matter the differences or preconceived notions—for God is a God of relationship. As we showed love to Little Buddy, others witnessed love being shown to a child who at first was shun. As we expressed love through our actions, others opened their hearts to our little buddy and accepted him.

What a beautiful testimony. God led Chad and Angela to their own "Samaria" and to their own "Zacchaeus." They surrendered to God's leading. They were intentional. They were relational. And they sought to be about the Father's business.

As witnesses for Jesus, may we grow to be more intentional in pursuing redemptive relationships with the lost—praying for, serving, and loving them in Jesus' name.

As His witnesses, may we grow to be more intentional in pointing people to Jesus for salvation.

As His witnesses, may we be about our Father's business.

What's Your Story

Before I became a believer in Jesus in 1987, I was interested in only one person's business—my own. Can you relate? In fact, I was the director, producer, and lead actor in the little story of me. I, Me, Mine—yes, it was all about me.

When God took hold of my life, I became a new creation in the Messiah. God gave me a completely new outlook on life: new motives, new perspective, new purpose, and may I add, a new game plan.

Interestingly, He also gave me new business to attend—His. What a thought. You know, as human beings our default mode in life is to look out for No. 1. Yet, when Jesus becomes our Lord and Savior, He becomes our No. 1 and His business comes first.

The story that preceded my salvation, the *Big Story of Me*, began a new chapter. He began writing the next chapter of my life. Now, instead of me being the writer, director, producer, and lead actor, the Lord is now running the show.

My new calling in life as a Christian is to play a bit role in the *Big Story of God*. In this new role I am to be first and foremost about the business of my Heavenly Father.

In my years as a college tennis coach, we had many players come through our program. And when they arrived on campus, everyone had to make a change. Now they would be playing tennis for something so much bigger than themselves—they were now playing on a team. When they stepped on that court, they were representatives of

East Tennessee State University. They represented the school, their teammates, coaches, and themselves. Ultimately when they competed they represented the school. Whether they won or lost a tennis match, the win or loss was credited to the team. And so, players had a responsibility to be about not only the business of playing and trying to win their match, but they also had a responsibility to represent the university, and represent it well in victory or defeat.

When we become believers we become a part of the church. As ambassadors, we represent our King. The change we make is that we no longer live for us, but for Him. So our lives are now lived for something way bigger than ourselves and represent the King in His court, this world.

Our testimony is the communication of how our story intersects with God's story. In other words, we're talking about our life narrative. It's important to understand our story and be able to articulate it to others as those doors of opportunity open.

One of the universal commonalities we human beings share is that we all have a story.

"So, what's your story?" I know, I know, that's a direct question and rather deep and comprehensive. If someone were to ask you that question, then what would you say? Certainly the context of the conversation would dictate your response.

In the context of our Christian witness, sharing our testimony is an important part of being about our Father's business. For it is good to share about His love and grace extended to us. The Bible tells us to "always be ready to give an answer to everyone who asks you to give the reason for the hope that is within you" (1 Peter 3:15).

Our testimony is how our story intersects with God's story. And a testimony is a powerful tool in the Master's hand as we communicate His love and grace to others. So it's important to understand and organize your story so you can appropriately articulate it or parts of it in conversation with others. Preparation is critical.

Preparing Your Testimony

In athletics, one of the keys to confidence is preparation. Before entering the court for a match, it's important to be prepared. Practice, practice, practice. Repetition, repetition, and so on. When we think of the biblical exhortation Peter gives us to always be ready, preparing our testimony is important. Readiness will come when we take time to pray and to write out a three-to-five minute testimony, not necessarily for the purposes of reciting it verbatim, but rather for the purpose of being able to access whatever part or parts of it to share at any particular moment as a conversation unfolds. In the context of conversation, you may share snippets of it and at other times there may be much more time to share about the difference the Lord has made in your life.

In preparing your testimony, here's a basic list of tips:

• Ask the Lord to give you wisdom and guidance in preparing and presenting your testimony.

• Always include life before Christ, the turning point (What made you seek? What happened (salvation)? What has Jesus meant in your life since that time?

• Always include the gospel. We're sinners separated from God. Jesus died for our sins and rose again, providing forgiveness of sin. We need to believe in Jesus for forgiveness and to enter into a personal relationship with God.

• Don't use Christian jargon. Words such as "born again," "convicted," "converted," do not communicate truth to the average non-Christian.

• Don't give the impression that the Christian life is a "bed of roses." Be genuine & authentic.

• Making an outline of your testimony is helpful.

• Memorize your testimony to give you confidence.

• As you share your testimony and become more comfortable doing so, you'll have the ability to flex and share different pieces at different times to different people as you feel inclined.

• Practice your testimony with a friend, getting feedback. Also, speaking your testimony aloud will allow you and others to get a better feel for how you're communicating. Sometimes a verbal expression of a thought or idea sounds much different than when it's read.

• Pray for opportunities to share your story.

Here's a simple way to think about content in forming the framework for your testimony. Pray through, meditate upon, then write down your story. There are three components that make up a believer's testimony:

Formation of God Paradigm (Before Christ): Head Knowledge

This is your formative or growing up years, or the time before you trusted in Christ. What kind of religious tradition, if any, did you grow up with? What was your understanding or belief about God? In my case, growing up in a Reform Temple, a liberal expression of Judaism, I always believed in God on some level and I believed He knew me and that I was special in His eyes. But we learned nothing about Jesus.

Experiencing His Grace (Trusting in Christ): Heart Knowledge

This is a moment or season in your life when faith in Jesus became personal. If you grew up in a Christian family environment, this is when your faith became your faith. It could be a time when you became serious about your faith and now wanted to live it out. As opposed to someone who didn't believe in Jesus on any level and came to a specific time of trusting in Him for forgiveness and eternal life.

The Consequences of Belief (Following Christ): Life Change

This is a critical piece of our story, for the difference Jesus has made in our life is the difference we want to share. For me, I experience abundant love, joy, and peace that transcend my circumstances, which frankly, at times, are quite painful. As I like to tell people, I follow the truth regardless of the consequences.

Once you put your testimony together, take some time and share it with someone and get their feedback. Practicing with a fellow believer initially will be easier. Their feedback will help you better understand how your testimony may resonate with others.

Remember, at the end of the day be ready to answer the question, "What's your story?"

As we think about the game plan of life in being about our Father's business, remember it's all about Him. He has a plan, a good plan noted in Jeremiah 29:11, "For I know the plans I have for you," declares the Lord, "to prosper you and not to harm you, plans to give you hope and a future" (NIV).

And what the Father's business is for each of us is unique and distinct. Yet, His desire for us in the evangelistic endeavor is to go where He wants and serve who He calls us to. You have a Samaria to go to, a Zacchaeus to serve. Where is it and who is it—that's for you to find out.

So seek His face and search out His game plan for life found in His Word. Then be about the great adventure of serving in His court, being about the Father's business.

Chapter 6
Training Session

SPIRITUAL MUSCLE MEMORY:
"And [Jesus] said to them, 'Why do you seek Me? Did you not know that I must be about My Father's business?'" (Luke 2:49).

WARM UP
Why is having a game plan essential to effective evangelism?

PRACTICE DRILLS
Why is it important to prepare and always be ready to share your testimony?

In the business of life's daily activities, what things can potentially take you away from the business of serving the lost in the evangelistic endeavor?

When you think about the business of your life, on a scale of 1-5 (5 being the greatest commitment), what priority are you placing on reaching out to the lost?

In what ways do you find the agenda-driven concept of relationships helpful in evangelism?

Ask God to show you what it will mean for you in practical terms to be more about "Your Father's business."

MATCH TIME
If you've never done so, put together a three-to-five minute written testimony, get with a believing friend, share your story and get feedback.

Pray for opportunities to tell your story or at least part of your story to an unbeliever.

EXTRA TRAINING
   Study Acts 26:1-32, 2 Corinthians 5:17-21

Part 2–Playing The Game

Chapter 7

First Serve

For we walk by faith, not by sight.
2 Corinthians 5:7

The first serve is potentially the most devastating stroke in the game. It can determine the outcome of a tennis match more than any other individual stroke. American Pete Sampras possessed one of the greatest serves in tennis history. At any time, he could come up with an ace during a tight service game or even late in a tiebreak. His placement and consistency were the best, yet he possessed much more than a big serve. He's considered one of the best players ever.

Sampras started on the professional tour in 1988 and competed in his last top-level tournament in 2002 when he won the US Open, defeating rival Andre Agassi in the final. He finished as the World No. 1 for six consecutive years (1993–1998), a record for the Open Era. Sampras' seven Wimbledon singles championships is an Open Era record shared by Roger Federer. Additionally, his five US Open singles titles is an Open Era record shared with both Federer and former World No. 1 player Jimmy Connors.

I had the privilege of seeing Sampras in person in August of 2002 at a professional tournament in Cincinnati. I watched his first round match with a good friend of mine, Tony. Sitting on the first row at one end of the court, we were as close to the court as you could be without being a ball boy. To see Sampras in action was a joy. And yes, the serve was most impressive in person.

One of the exciting things about a tennis match is you never know what's going to happen. It may be quick, decisive, boring, and last less than an hour. Or it may be a protracted, exciting match lasting several hours. No matter how much one trains and prepares, what transpires on the court during a match can be surprising and unpredictable. You never know what's going to happen.

But whatever occurs on the court, the beginning point of a tennis match is always the first serve. In competitive tennis, it's a ritual to raise the ball to your opponent before the first serve of the match, indicating practice serves are complete and the match is beginning. This serve is for real. Match on.

Once that first serve is struck, anything can happen. Each point can take a life of its own and each match the same. Tennis can be very unpredictable. A tennis match in one sense is a walk of faith.

If you're a tennis player, you understand. If you don't play, please have faith in what I'm saying.

Evangelism is a walk of faith. When we enter the Court of King Jesus—the world He has made and the sphere of influence in which He's placed us—our evangelistic effort is a faith venture.

Not having it all figured out and not really knowing how it will turn out is okay. It's all part of the process. Pleasing God in our witness, just as in all areas of life, is a faith issue. Because "without faith, it's impossible to please God" (Hebrews 11:6). When our hearts are aligned with God, we will be more inclined to walk by faith and take our witness into the world. Interestingly, the "walking" and "going" are going to be different for each of us.

To be honest, when we step onto the court of the King as His servants (in the arena of evangelism), we don't know what's going to happen. Events unfold in real-time, often in unpredictable fashion.

When we break it down to the most basic principle—in the evangelistic endeavor our *going* is the same as *following* Jesus. He will take you where He wants you to be. What you will do and what you will say will also be an act of faith in following Him. Have confidence in Him.

An appropriate starting prayer is: "Lord, please increase my faith in this area of personal evangelism and help me follow You where you call me to go."

Abraham's Call to Go

When God called Abraham out of the city of Ur and told him to leave everything he knew—his family, his country—to go to a land that God would show him, Abraham went.

Now the Lord had said to Abram: "Get out of our country, from your family and from your father's house, to a land that I will show you. I will make you a great nation; I will bless you and make your name great; And you shall be a blessing. I will bless those who bless you, and I will curse him who curses you; And in you all the families of the earth shall be blessed. So Abram departed as the Lord had spoken to him..."(Genesis 12:1-4).

Simple, yet so profound and life-changing. This call was so transformative that God gave Abram a new name, indicating a new season and a new purpose in his life. Abram became Abraham.

We don't see Abram questioning the Lord: "Lord, can you give me a map? What's it going to be like there? Can you elaborate a bit? I want to know what I'm getting myself into here." No, he simply followed.

Joshua's Marching Orders

Joshua was born in Egyptian slavery, trained under Moses and by God's choice rose to the key position of leading Israel into the Promised Land.

Just before Moses died, he passed the baton of leadership to Joshua. Joshua was nearly ninety years old when he became Israel's leader. At this point Israel was at the end of its forty year wandering period.

After Moses died, God commissioned Joshua to lead the Israelites into the Promised Land: "Moses My servant is dead. Now therefore, arise, go over this Jordan, you and all this people, to the land, which I am giving to them—the children of Israel" (Joshua 1:2).

The time had come for God to fulfill His covenant with Abraham and give Israel the Promised Land. Joshua was God's man for God's task in God's time to lead God's people. But it wouldn't be easy. Although Joshua was a brave warrior and had displayed courage in the past, he would again need strength and courage for this task.

Three times in Joshua 1, God commands Joshua to be strong and courageous. For example, in Joshua 1:9 God says, "Have I not commanded you? Be strong and of good courage; do not be afraid, nor be dismayed, for the Lord your God is with you wherever you go."

In his case, Joshua had a clear understanding of what he needed to do and how he needed to do it. The challenge for him was faith. He needed strength and courage for the task. And God was faithful.

Not only did the Lord tell Joshua to be strong and courageous, but He also told him that He would be with him wherever he traveled. That is key for us as we walk by faith in the evangelistic adventure. God is with us wherever we go.

So when God does show you where to go and what to do, know He is with you every step of the way. And He is faithful.

Fishing for Men

Jesus said to Simon (called Peter) and his brother Andrew: "Follow Me and I will make you fishers of men" (Matthew 4:18). Jesus didn't explain to these Galilean fishermen what that statement meant. They simply followed. Jesus had encountered Peter and Andrew before, near Bethabara, in the Jordan region, where Andrew (and perhaps Peter as well) had become a disciple of John the Baptist. In this Matthew 4 passage, Jesus is calling them to follow Him in long-term discipleship. Their decision to follow would mean three-and-a-half years spending lots of time with the Lord. During that time they underwent a life-changing process where they were transformed from fishers of fish to fishers of men as Jesus taught them, set an example for them, and allowed opportunities for them to minister. There were also times to debrief following ministry activities.

They would become vessels of His grace, His ambassadors of reconciliation, His witnesses of the Kingdom.

God calls us to follow Him as we engage in the evangelistic endeavor. As we follow Him, He will transform us and will show us the way we need to go. He will give us the grace we need for the work. "And God is able to make all grace abound to you, so that in all things, at all times, having all that you need, you will abound in every good work" (2 Corinthians 9:8).

In our lives we have comfortable ways of being and living. Just as Peter and Andrew would have been very comfortable and familiar with fishing for fish, so we also are comfortable and familiar in areas of our life.

Yet, the call to walk by faith in our personal witness requires we be open to God as He molds us and changes us from what we are to what He wants us to be.

What did Peter and Andrew know about fishing for men? They knew well the fishing trade and God used what they knew to make them witnesses for Him.

It seems to me in Jesus' wordplay that the transformative principle is the "for men" part. Peter and Andrew knew fishing. Jesus would reorient their fishing trade to include the relational component.

This reorientation was not so much about what they did, but rather *why* and *for whom* they did it.

Because Jesus came to seek and to save the lost, His focal point was people. People would become Peter and Andrew's focus too.

I was still coaching tennis when I became a Christian. My Kingdom orientation following my salvation included coaching tennis to glorify Jesus, not simply helping people become better tennis players.

And you? What are your passions, gifts, and abilities? Will you surrender them to Jesus and allow Him to mold them for His Glory to accomplish His Kingdom purposes, which center on redeeming lost people?

"Becoming a fisher of men doesn't necessarily entail leaving your job or ignoring your gifts, abilities and passions. Rather, it's about your willingness to subjugate them all the Lord, allowing Him to transform you into the witness He desires you to become. "

While it could entail leaving a job, becoming a fisher of men ultimately is about reorientation of purpose. So, whatever you do, whether it be tennis, fishing, or something else—do it for God's glory as His witness.

To Boldly Go Where No Man Has Gone Before

Jesus spent His entire earthly ministry within the boundaries of the Holy Land. Yet after the resurrection, He commanded His followers to make disciples of all nations, "All authority has been given to Me in heaven and on earth. Go therefore and make disciples of all nations, baptizing them in the name of the Father and of the Son and of the Holy Spirit, teaching them to observe all things that I have commanded you; and lo, I am with you always, even to the end of the age" (Matthew 28:18-20). Notice the first word: "Go." We can only imagine their reaction when He said go out to all nations.

The resurrected Lord reaffirmed His mandate to go to all nations in Acts 1:8, including the promise of the Holy Spirit partnership in the Great Commission endeavor: "But you shall receive power when the Holy Spirit has come upon you; and you shall be witnesses to Me in Jerusalem, and in all Judea and Samaria and to the end of the earth."

I wonder what the disciples were thinking when they heard the words "to the end of the earth." The disciples are a great example of stepping out on faith. They were called to move beyond the walls of everything they knew.

Geography was only one part of the story. They would follow the Lord to new places, but they would also be ministering among various peoples and cultures. This would be quite a learning experience and faith stretching endeavor to be sure.

The willingness to go where you've never gone before—and maybe even do what you've never done before—is an amazing commitment. This was the Great Commission given to the disciples and it is the same mandate for us today. Will you step out in faith and go where He calls?

The Question that Changed My Life

Being an assistant tennis coach at East Tennessee State University in the mid-90s gave me very flexible summers. I had known about the ministry of Jews for Jesus for several years and had determined to participate in *Summer Campaign* in 1997. Summer Campaign was a six-week ministry that focused on street evangelism. The program would entail a two-week training in Chicago at Moody Bible Institute and then four weeks on the streets of the Big Apple—New York City. I had never handed out a gospel track in my life, yet I wanted to apply for a position on the ministry team.

The team recruiter, a man named Stephen, noticed that I had listed guitar as a hobby on my application. He asked if I'd be interested in also applying for a position on the mobile evangelistic music team of the ministry called The Liberated Wailing Wall. It was a traveling ministry team that proclaimed the gospel through music, drama, and testimony in churches and on Christian college campuses. We also did evangelistic outreaches on secular college campuses and in big cities. If you're wondering what the presentations were like, picture in your mind *Fiddler on the Roof* meets Jesus.

I had seen this music team when it came through Tennessee and they were very talented. I reminded Stephen that I listed "guitar" as a *hobby*. I could play basic chords and occasionally led worship during our singles group at church and at campus fellowship. You know, songs like "Shine Jesus Shine" with very simple chord progressions. "I'm not a musician."

Stephen then posed a question that rocked my world and if you are honest, will rock yours. He said, "Are you willing to make yourself available to God?" After processing what he was saying, I did a double take. I didn't say, "Sure, what do you have for me?" Or better, "What does God have for me?" No, I said something like, "Available for what?" He challenged me to pray about applying for a position on the music team. That was the spring of 1996.

I wrestled with the question for a couple of months. Finally, I decided to apply. I had Jim, my church's music minister, record three songs I had the most confidence in performing. I had never recorded a demo tape before. After sending my application for the music team to Jews for Jesus in the fall, I chuckled and thought, "I'm no musician."

In December, I received a call from Stephen. "Congratulations. You've been accepted to Summer Campaign *and* you've been accepted for a position on the Liberated Wailing Wall. Pack your bags. You're moving." I was shocked.

With one phone call, that six-week, short-term ministry trip turned into a two-year, full-time ministry commitment. I moved from Johnson City, Tennessee in June 1997 with no more than a twenty-nine inch hard shell suitcase, a book bag, and my guitar. During that time God transformed my life.

I served on the short-term evangelism team that summer, then worked five months in San Francisco preparing for a seventeen-month tour of ministry with the music team. For fifteen months I toured North America, then spent two months touring internationally, which included stops in England, South Africa, and Australia.

That two-year ministry commitment in the late 1990s was life-changing for me and my wife Lori, whom I met during that time. After taking a three-year break from vocational ministry, we went to New York City where I served from 2003 to 2009 as a missionary to my Jewish people.

And how did it all start? By simply answering, "Yes.", to the profound, life-transforming question: "Are you willing to make yourself available to God?"

I don't know what that challenge means for you today, and certainly don't know what "Yes" will mean for you, yet the question remains. What will your answer be?

A Picture of "Going"

"Going out" looks different for each of us. "Going" can mean many different things. Yet we're all called to follow Jesus and walk by faith.

What going looks like to you may include:
Praying more faithfully for a missionary or mission work (Matt. 9:35-39).
Praying God would bring unbelievers into your life.
Befriending an unbeliever in your sphere of influence.
Serving in an outreach activity with your home church.
Leaving everything you know and heading to a mission field in a new place, like Chad and Angela.

Going might be joining a local group or organization where you can express your gifts and passions while being salt and light. Consider Joan's story:

During the years that I led the women's ministries at my church, I had a growing conviction that though I loved serving the women and saw some trust in Christ as Savior, my time was totally absorbed around women and families with some church connection. After leaving the church staff, God gave me a desire to rub shoulders with those outside the church, and explore how I could share my faith and grow myself. That opportunity came when I was first asked to serve on the Homeowners Association Board (HOA), then as president of our condominium complex. That was an investment of time and effort that rather intimidated me, but I felt sure it was God's response to my prayer for His direction.

It was challenging, for sure. But through the two years I was involved, I felt humbled at the open doors to form friendships, some which continue on. I was able to guide the board through some conflict resolution on disagreements which brought several to talk to me about difficulties in their own lives. It was delightful to come to know several who were believers. In one instance, I felt God's prompting to do a loving thing for a lesbian couple—to show them Christ's love—which brought an amazing reaction. Though they've not yet trusted in Jesus, showing them God's love opened a door. I found that people do not usually refuse to have you pray for a particular burden that they have.

What an adventure with God and growth in faith.

Walking by faith means lots of things including the willingness to take risks and face rejection, along with accepting the unknowns.

As His servants, we can know our King's motives are the very best for us and others. And we are called to do His bidding. When He says go, go. In tennis, when we step onto the court, we can never know what's going to happen. Yet one constant that should give us confidence is knowing we have prepared.

In the evangelistic adventure, this knowledge should give us confidence:

We know the King.

We know He's in control.

We know He seeks the best for us and others.

We know our resources.

We know the need.

We know our responsibility to be a witness.

What don't we know?

How it's all going to work.

What exactly is going to happen.

So let's make ourselves available to God. And when we hear Him say, "Whom shall I send, And who will go for us?"—May our answer echo the words of the prophet Isaiah when he replied, "Here am I Lord—send me" (Isaiah 6:8).

So, are you ready? Good. "First Serve."

Chapter 7
Training Session

SPIRITUAL MUSCLE MEMORY
"For we walk by faith, not by sight" (2 Corinthians 5:7)

WARM UP
Why is it important to approach personal evangelism as a faith venture?

PRACTICE DRILLS
What or who has been an inspiring example to you of someone walking by faith in the area of personal evangelism? Why so?

Why is faith vital to engaging the evangelistic process?

Besides evangelism, what other challenging endeavors in your life have involved a process of walking by faith? Discuss.

MATCH TIME
What will your walk by faith in the area of personal evangelism look like for you in this season of your life?

Pray, "Lord, please increase my faith in the area of my personal witness. Amen."

EXTRA TRAINING
Study Hebrews 11:1–40

Chapter 8

Facing Fear

For God has not given us a Spirit of fear,
but of power and love and of a sound mind.
2 Timothy 1:7

Cramps. They are the physical menace every competitive tennis player fears. They are caused by lactic acid in muscles, dehydration, or a loss of mineral content in the body like low calcium, potassium, or magnesium. Severe cramps may so debilitate a player that he or she will have trouble moving. In some cases, cramps may cause a player to quit.

The scene is the 1989 French Open. The match is one of the most memorable in tennis history. Seventeen-year-old American Michael Chang faced top-ranked Ivan Lendl in a fourth round (round of sixteen) match. Lendl had already two French Open titles on his résumé and was looking for a third.

Steven Pye frames the scene quite well:

> At the end of the fourth set, Chang started varying his shots from the baseline, taking the pace off the ball and playing numerous 'moon shots.' Chang explains: "Toward the end of the fourth set, I started to cramp anytime I had to run really hard. So I resorted to hitting a lot of moon balls, and trying to keep points as short as possible. If I had an opportunity to go for a winner, I'd

go for it."

Over three-and-a-half hours on court had taken its toll on Chang, his calves and thighs tightening up under the strain, greatly restricting his freedom of movement. Although Chang immediately broke Lendl in the fifth set, his dehydration was such that he tried desperately to play catch-up, drinking water and consuming bananas at increasingly regular intervals to fix the problem. It was starting to look like a fight that the youngster was losing.

At 2-1 up in the final set, Chang couldn't move. What had at first threatened to be a classic French Open match, looked as if it would end in a whimper. Indeed, such was the extent of Chang's immobility that he walked towards the umpire's chair with the intention of calling an end to proceedings.

"I was really close to quitting," Chang admitted later. "I started to say to myself: 'Who am I kidding here? I'm 17 years old and I'm playing against the No1 player in the world. It wouldn't be so bad to just call it a day.'"

But something struck Chang at his lowest moment, a sense that quitting wasn't an option. "When I got to the service line, I got an unbelievable conviction of heart. Looking back, I really feel like it was the Lord kind of telling me, 'Michael, what do you think you're doing here?' If I quit once, the second, third, fourth, or fifth time that I am faced with that kind of circumstance, that kind of difficulty, I'm going to quit again." Win or lose, Chang was going to fight until the end.[5]

In the middle of the decisive fifth set, Michael Chang did the unthinkable—he hit an underhand serve. This is unconventional, even for the recreational player. For a professional it is unfathomable, but legal. Chang won that point and went on to win the match. American tennis pro Todd Martin, a contemporary of Chang's, once described that underhand serve as "...the last stone that felled Goliath."[6]

Amazingly, Chang went on to win the tournament, becoming the youngest French Open champion in history.

This truly was an exhibition in boldness and courage.

In the spiritual life of a Jesus follower, fear, whether real or imagined, is one emotion we all face. When engaged in personal evangelism, our fear may become so debilitating that it may cause us to quit or never engage the process.

Fear takes many forms. There is fear of rejection, fear of not knowing what to say or do, fear of saying or doing the wrong thing, fear of not being in control, fear of the unknown, fear of _____—you fill in the blank.

Jesus knows our fears. In fact, He knows them perfectly and fully. He is God and knows all things. Perhaps that's why He repeats these two words more often than any other phrase in the gospels: "Fear not."

Let us acknowledge that fear is a reality in the personal evangelistic endeavor—and for good reason. First of all, we're in a spiritual war as we've discussed earlier and there are weapons working against us. Next, the gospel message is polarizing and will create a strong reaction when clearly communicated, both positive and negative. Finally, rejection is not just a possibility; it is a probability.

Aside from that, we've got nothing to fear.

So, let's be upfront and say that dealing with fear may not make fear subside. The goal needs to be the willingness to go where He leads and do what He wants in spite of what we feel. Courage is doing what God calls us to do in spite of our fear. Courage is not the absence of fear; it is conquest of fear.

Here's a powerful question that will frame the issue and help us grapple at the crossroads of faith and fear: "Do I believe their salvation is more important than my safety?"

The answer to that question will shape our evangelistic efforts, because the personal evangelistic process is risky business. Let's not fool ourselves. At the same time, we have all the resources we need to engage in the battle, to overcome fear (not eradicate it), and to be victorious in our witness.

God calls us to be faithful to His evangelistic calling, and because we are individual servants of the King, serving in His court will look different for each of us. I'm not you and you're not me.

We are His, and as such, we are simply called to sow and water as He leads. It is God's prerogative to give the increase. It's also His prerogative to allow rejection.

The Fear Factor

Soon after I became a believer, I called a good friend of mine, Greg, who was a powerful witness in my journey to faith. I told him I'd become a Christian, and he said, "Great. You've got to tell your family."

"What?"

He said, "You must tell your family."

I confess I was a "closet Christian" for eighteen months. It took that long for me to "come out." Over those eighteen agonizing months, I went from one family member to another, sharing my new found faith in Jesus. Being Jewish and the first believer in my family, I had no idea what the response would be. One's imagination can paralyze a person.

But you know what? Despite the various responses of acceptance, peaceful resignation, confusion, misunderstandings, and threats to not tell other family members, it turned out okay.

I have learned in my Christian life, like many things in life, that thinking about doing certain things can create much more angst than the reality of doing it—like going to the doctor, or dentist. Similarly, I believe the thought of doing personal evangelism produces much more anxiety than actually doing it.

If you think I'm immune to fear because I'm writing this book, think again. We shouldn't fear our responsibilities in any area of life, including the arena of personal evangelism.

I've experienced fear in sharing my faith with my family, sharing the gospel on the street and over the phone, and even during personal visits in cafés, apartments, and homes. I've even experienced fear in asking an unbeliever to hang out and get a cup of coffee with the purpose of simply getting to know them.

The issue isn't whether I will experience the emotion of fear. Rather, will I allow fear to paralyze me, keeping me from doing what God calls, or will fear simply be an obstacle to overcome?

In personal evangelism, we could sort fear into three basic categories: unsettling fear, debilitating fear, and paralyzing fear.

Unsettling fears are those uncomfortable sensations we feel prior to or in the midst of doing the work of evangelism. One time I was in the middle of sharing my faith with an unbelieving family member. In the midst of our conversation, this person rightly stated, "If I understand you correctly, the gospel message means that if I reject Jesus, then I am hell bound. Is that correct?" It took a few seconds for me to process the question before answering, "Yes, that's correct." Those few seconds were filled with unsettling fear.

Debilitating fear may not completely disable us from doing what God calls us to do, but certainly impedes or hampers the effort. I think debilitating fear kept me from telling my own family about my new found faith in Jesus. As I mentioned, it took me eighteen months to share with my entire family, but I eventually did.

Paralyzing fear is the kind of fear that completely disables us from engaging in the task God has called us to. During the summer of 1997 I was just beginning my first street evangelistic effort with Jews for Jesus called "Summer Campaign." I was in the big city, New York, and my team and I were in a busy area of Manhattan one night. My team leader looked at me as we were getting ready to take our positions to hand out gospel literature and said, "Larry, go over to that crowd of people standing in the line at that movie theater across the street and tell them about Jesus. There are people there who need Jesus." It's hard to describe my fear. For a few minutes I decided it just wasn't going to happen. However, I did get over it, engaged the group and it was fine.

Fear is a feeling, an emotion. Sometimes fear is real; other times it is a creation of the mind. And I don't know about you, but sometimes my imagination runs wild.

Feelings come and go, yet we're called to walk by faith in spite of what our feelings may tell us. It's kind of like physical training. If I worked out whenever I felt like it, I would rarely work out. I work out because I've made a decision to work out. It's not based on feeling, but on a commitment.

Tennis players don't train only when they feel like it. They train on a regimen, because they've made the commitment to engage. That commitment overcomes any feeling.

While a high school sophomore in Florida, I spent a good portion of the school year waking up twice a week at 4:15 a.m. to train before classes. A teammate picked me up and we went to a public tennis facility, turned on the lights, practiced, and then ran on the track to finish up. That happened only one year mind you, but it was a case of a commitment overcoming a feeling—a feeling of sleepiness.

In our commitment to witness for Jesus, the feeling we need to overcome is fear. Fear is real. Don't deny it. Deal with it.

The Reality of Rejection

In the game of tennis, losing is probably the closest thing I can connect to rejection we experience in the endeavor of evangelism. Losing stings and every competitive player has to learn to process this reality. Losing is a real possibility every time a player steps on the court. No matter your level of accomplishment, losing is part of the process of playing tennis. And in our evangelistic efforts, rejection is part of the process.

In fact, rejection is part of the Christian life just as Jesus said it would be. The first time Jesus spoke in public He said:

"Blessed are those who are persecuted for righteousness' sake, for theirs is the kingdom of heaven. Blessed are you when they revile and persecute you, and say all kinds of evil against you falsely for My sake. Rejoice and be exceedingly glad, for great is your reward in heaven, for so they persecuted the prophets who were before you" (Matthew 5:10-12).

And just before He was arrested He addressed the disciples with these words:

"If the world hates you, you know that it hated Me before it hated you. If you were of the world, the world would love its own. Yet because you are not of the world, but I chose you out of the world, therefore the world hates you. Remember the word that I said to you, 'A servant is not greater than his master.' If they persecuted Me, they will also persecute you" (John 15:18-20).

The Apostle Paul added: "All who desire to live godly in Christ Jesus will suffer persecution" (2 Timothy 3:12).

Jesus experienced rejection. As His followers, we should also expect rejection.

But rejection is not just an unwelcome aspect of the Christian life. It's the pathway to fully identify with our Lord. As believers we long for and gravitate toward the positive benefits of following Jesus: forgiveness of sin, abundant and eternal life, love, joy and peace that transcends our circumstances, purpose, and more. Yet our identification with the Lord is not only about identifying with Him in His victory, it's about identifying with Him in His sorrow. He was, as the Bible states, a "Man of sorrows and acquainted with grief" (Isaiah 53:3).

On a human level, we may want to avoid persecution and rejection. Yet on a spiritual level, this is a key component on the road to deepest communion with God. Paul noted, "For as the sufferings of Christ abound in us, so our consolation also abounds through Christ" (2 Corinthians 1:5). Specifically, personal evangelism provides a platform for rejection to take place.

Like most people, I like to be liked. I like people and am not the kind of person that will say, "Alienation, misunderstanding, rejection by others—count me in." No, in my flesh, in my humanness, I'm saying, "Count me out." How about you?

Think about this for a moment: Imagine your Christian testimony is rejected by everyone you encounter except one person who didn't shun you. They were attracted to you, to Christ in you and wanted to know more. And what if, in the midst of that rejection by all others, this one person not only wanted to hear the gospel, but made a decision to trust in Christ for salvation? Would it be worthwhile?

Jesus said, "There is joy in the presence of the angels of God over one sinner who repents" (Luke 15:10).

Yes, rejection is part of the process... but so is rejoicing. Praise God.

Coping Mechanisms

I'm going to be a bit transparent here about my tennis playing career. If you're a tennis player, you'll be able to relate. If not, I hope you'll be able to relate.

I was saved at age twenty-three. My faith, my confidence and my foundation are found in Jesus, my Rock and my Redeemer. Unfortunately, my tennis playing career, at least my junior and college careers, ended when I was nineteen years old. Looking back I believe if I knew the Lord during that season of life I would have been much better equipped to deal with the fear of losing—a competitive equivalent of rejection in my eyes at the time. I was mentally fragile as a competitive player. There were times I was what we call in tennis circles a "mental midget." I didn't cope well with the pressure of a tennis match and the prospect of losing. My fear of losing was often debilitating and affected my performance.

Later, as a teaching professional at clubs and academies, and also as college tennis coach, I would occasionally compete in a tennis tournament. And you know what? My faith in Christ allowed me to enjoy the process of playing and competing—regardless of the result. My identity wasn't completely wrapped up in winning or losing a match. Rather, my faith in Jesus gave me a healthy perspective on coping with the potential reality of losing a tennis match.

You see, a healthy perspective makes a huge difference in athletics and in the evangelistic endeavor.

One needs to be able to cope. In tennis, part of coping includes dealing with the potential of losing, and for some players, dealing with the fear of losing. In our witness, the coping has to do with potential rejection. And how will we cope? By knowing "Whose we are" and knowing "Who we are" in Christ. Also knowing the importance of sharing the gospel and the need of precious people to hear this life saving message provides a healthy perspective.

We need our faith strengthened. As we've noted, "Faith comes by hearing and hearing by the word of God" (Romans 10:17). Prayer is also a mechanism by which we can cope with whatever comes our way. In addition, fellowship with other like-minded believers is also a source of strength.

Another powerful way to cope with fear is to memorize God's Word. Here are three verses that can help:

Isaiah 26:3. "You will keep him in perfect peace, whose mind is stayed on You, because he trusts in You."

2 Timothy 1:7. "For God has not given us a spirit of fear, but of power, and of love, and of a sound mind."

Philippians 4:6-7. "Be anxious for nothing, but in everything by prayer and supplication with thanksgiving, let your requests be known to God and the peace of God that surpasses all understanding will guard your hearts and minds in Christ Jesus."

We have a great example of dealing with fear from the book of Acts. After healing a lame man and preaching the gospel at the Temple (Acts 3), Peter and John are arrested (Acts 4). They are interrogated by the Sanhedrin and commanded not to speak in Jesus' name again. After saying that they must speak in Jesus' name, Peter and John are released under great threats. And what do they do? They join the believers and pray for boldness. In verse 29, they pray, "Now, Lord look on their threats, and grant your servants that with all boldness they may speak Your word."

They got their answer: "And when they had prayed, the place where they were assembled together was shaken and they were all filled with the Holy Spirit and they spoke the word with great boldness" (Acts 4:31).

The threats didn't change. The risk didn't change. They simply prayed.

And just a tidbit from that passage I think remarkable: Acts 4:13 reads, "Now when they saw the boldness of Peter and John, and perceived that they were uneducated and untrained men, they marveled. And they realized that they had been with Jesus."

In the area of personal evangelism, do you feel unqualified? Are you uneducated and untrained? Good, you'll do just fine. Spend time with Jesus as did the disciples. There is no way to overemphasize the power of prayer and the power of God's Word—the power in spending time with Jesus. Simple, yes. Profound, yes. Easy, no.

The peace and perspective to engage in personal evangelism in general and deal with fear and rejection specifically will come through His Word, prayer, and fellowship.

Jesus said we could do nothing without Him, but in Him and through Him we can do all things He calls us to do. Yes, "I can do all things through Christ who strengthens me" (Philippians 4:13).

Even the Apostle Paul proclaimed the gospel in spite of fear. Now if anyone demonstrated boldness and courage, it was Paul. Yet he wrote in 2 Corinthians 7:5, "For indeed, when we came to Macedonia, our bodies had no rest, but we were troubled on every side. Outside were conflicts, inside were fears."

Readiness: A Key to Confidence

Preparation plays a key role in the confidence of any athlete. This basic principle applies to many disciplines in life, including personal evangelism.

Tennis players who train for competitive tournaments engage in a variety of activities. Physical preparation includes lifting weights, running, jumping rope, stretching, and agility exercises; various on-court drills, practice sets and matches; mental exercises and visualization; and for some there is a nutritional program, which may include a whole set of supplements. All of this in order to do one thing: to help the player perform to their highest potential.

In addition to things we've already mentioned like prayer, fellowship and Bible study, there are also a variety of other activities we can engage in to make us better witnesses. There are books to read, seminars to attend, equipping classes, and DVDs or CDs on the topic. Fellowship with like-minded Christians who have a heart to reach the lost can be productive— "As iron sharpens iron, so one brother sharpens another" (Proverbs 27:17). Additionally, online chat rooms are a locale where you can observe and engage in lots of witnessing conversations.

A final and perhaps most important component for building confidence in witnessing is simply experience. The readiness component is strengthened through trial and error—yes—error. When we remember we can't turn somebody off that the Holy Spirit is turning on, we can have confidence to practice the engagement of evangelism without the fear that our messing up will keep someone out of the Kingdom.

Doctors practice medicine, attorneys practice law, and as believers, we are in the practice of evangelism.

The interesting thing is that we are already witnesses for Jesus. The only issue is what kind of witnesses will we be. Whether we realize it or not, we have a testimony. How effective or engaged is that testimony? God knows.

I have a friend named Gordon, whom I've known since the early 1990s. At that time he was a seminary student thinking about medical school. Becoming a doctor was first an idea. Then over time, it became a reality. But it was a process. There were entrance exams, getting through medical school, then going through residency and finally, becoming a full-fledged physician and earning the legal right to practice medicine.

Evangelism is a process where God has already accepted us into His family and made us official ambassadors of reconciliation. Not only do we have a mandate to be His witnesses, we also have the right to "practice" evangelism.

And this practice will entail making mistakes, falling, getting up, and continuing.

I remember witnessing to Jonathan, a Jewish man who lived in the Upper West Side of Manhattan in New York City. I would visit him every couple of weeks sharing the good news of Messiah. During one visit I wanted to show him the existence of Satan in the Old Testament. I used allusions to Satan's existence from the prophets

Isaiah and Ezekiel. Not my best choice. Why didn't I simply take him to the book of Job, where we see God and Satan clearly having conversations? At the time I was an experienced missionary. I should have known better. But you know what—it was and is okay. You see, when I became an ordained minister of the gospel, I had the right to "practice" missionary work. And with that right would come the right to make mistakes.

So wherever you are in the process, it's okay. Whether reading this book makes you nervous or you are an experienced missionary, or somewhere in between, God is more than able to help you grow more into the witness He desires you to be.

Practicing tennis, or medicine, or ministry, or evangelism requires a willingness to make mistakes.

Along the way, something develops. It's called confidence. The kind of confidence that comes with doing, with making mistakes, and seeing fruit that God gives along the way.

Jesus said, "And whatever you ask in My name, that will I do, that the Father may be glorified in the Son. If you ask anything in My name, I will do it" (John 14:13-14).

It is God's will for us to engage in the evangelistic process and be His witnesses. It's His will to grant us the courage and boldness to fulfill our individual roles in that process as He builds His church.

So the question isn't whether He will or won't give us boldness and courage in the midst of fear. The question is will we ask for it? Yes, it may take faith, and perhaps a portion of boldness and courage to pray for the same.

Let us pray for boldness and courage in spite of fear and in spite of whatever feelings or circumstances, either real or imagined, that oppose our witness. I'm confident He will meet us at our point of need. Fear not, forge ahead, and walk boldly and courageously, telling of His wondrous works—for people need the Lord.

Chapter 8
Training Session

SPIRITUAL MUSCLE MEMORY

"For God has not given us a Spirit of fear, but of power and love and of a sound mind" (2 Timothy 1:7).

WARM UP

Regarding evangelism, what are your biggest fears and how do they affect the sharing of your faith?

PRACTICE DRILLS

When in the past have you displayed boldness and courage in any area of life? What enabled you to face that challenge?

What do boldness and courage look like in your personal witness?

MATCH TIME

What will you do to face your fears and walk in boldness and courage?

EXTRA TRAINING

Study Acts 4:1-31
.

Chapter 9

Friend or Foe

You shall love your neighbor as yourself.
Matthew 22:39

Chris Evert and Martina Navratilova had a tremendous fifteen-year rivalry from 1973 to 1988, playing eighty matches against one another. It is considered to be one of the top rivalries in tennis history and in sports in general. During that time Evert was ranked No. 1 in the world seven times, while Navratilova matched that feat, also finishing No. 1 seven times. They were the top two female players of that era.

Paul McElhinney summed it up this way: "Navratilova and Evert untypically, were able to combine a friendship off the court, which would have been almost inconceivable at the top of the men's game at the time.

Theirs was a rivalry of opposites. Evert was the cool 'Ice Maiden,' graceful, controlled and disciplined, a baseline supremo. Navratilova, by contrast, was powerful, explosive, strong on the serve and at the net. One was a right-hander and the other a left-hander. One was the all-American girl from the Sunshine State, the other the outsider from Communist Czechoslovakia (although a virulent critic of the Communist regime who eventually took citizenship in the US). These acknowledged contrasts simply added to the spice of their intense rivalry on court. They were a female equivalent of that equally intense rivalry between Lendl and McEnroe of the same era. In their head to head encounters, Navratilova came out on top by 43 wins to 37."[7]

There are certainly rivalries in sports, friendly and otherwise. But in the game of life on the court of this world, believers have no human rival as we seek to reach all people with the gospel of Jesus Christ.

Interestingly, it is in the context of relationships where personal evangelism takes place. Yes, we're in a battle, but as we've learned, our battle is not with flesh and blood. Rather, it's spiritual in nature. Jesus said some interesting things about human adversaries, even human "enemies."

Jesus was called a friend of sinners and told His followers to love all people, including our enemies, the same way He did. This is the nature of relationships in God's Kingdom. The Lord elaborates:

"You have heard that it was said, 'You shall love your neighbor and hate your enemy.' But I say to you, love your enemies, bless those who curse you, do good to those who hate you, and pray for those who spitefully use you and persecute you, that you may be sons of your Father in heaven; for He makes His sun rise on the evil and on the good, and sends rain on the just and on the unjust. For if you love those who love you, what reward have you? Do not even the tax collectors do the same? And if you greet your brethren only, what do you do more than others? Do not even the tax collectors do so? Therefore you shall be perfect, just as your Father in heaven is perfect" (Matthew 5:43-48).

When Jesus was asked in Matthew 23:36 what the greatest commandment was, He responded, "'You shall love the LORD your God with all your heart, with all your soul, and with all your mind.' This is the first and greatest commandment. And the second is like it: 'You shall love your neighbor as yourself.' On these two commandments hang all the Law and the Prophets" (Matthew 22:37-40).

In the realm of our personal witness to others, what do we make of Jesus' commandment to "love your neighbor as yourself"?

In one sense it speaks of relationship. We can't love someone we don't know. The phrase: "You shall love your neighbor as yourself" is a direct quote from Leviticus 19:18. In fact, it is the most quoted Old Testament text in the entire New Testament (see also Matthew 5:43, 19:19; Mark 12:31, 33; Luke 10:27; Romans 13:9; Galatians 5:14; James 2:8). When God repeats Himself, you can be sure it's very important.

Jesus, in declaring the greatest commandments, communicates the centrality of relationships—relationship with God and relationship with others.

Entering Intentional Relationships

Relationships and personal evangelism go hand in hand. Personal evangelism is personal—pun intended. Relationships that are intentional are the platform on which the process occurs.

In his book *Eats with Sinners*, Arron Chambers writes: "Relationships are the key to reaching lost people. I define evangelism as 'an intentional relationship through which someone is introduced to Jesus Christ.' Healthy relationships are essential if we want to have the kind of life God intended for all of us, and they are also essential if we want to reach lost people like Jesus did."[8]

Chambers adds, "An intentional relationship for a Christian is one in which a person intends to—one day—have the chance to introduce another person to Jesus and then one day—does introduce him or her to Jesus."[9]

A survey conducted by Church Growth, Inc. revealed what should be obvious: most people come to a saving faith in Jesus through an intentional relationship. They asked more than 10,000 people, "What was most responsible for your coming to Christ and this church?"[10] Seventy-nine percent responded, "A friend or relative invited me."

Intentional relationships are key to the evangelistic process. Jesus was asked why He shared a meal with tax collectors and sinners. He responded, "Those who are well have no need of a physician, but those who are sick. I have come not to call the righteous, but sinners to repentance" (Luke 5:30-32).

Jesus, the Great Physician, is a friend of sinners. Since I am a sinner saved by His grace I'm certainly glad about that.

Relationships are Difficult, Messy, and Worth It

It was in the context of relationship that the Lord ministered to people. That may seem obvious and even self-evident in principle, but in practice, we know relationships can be messy and difficult. There are no guarantees regarding the response of another to Jesus. With that said, we then understand why at times we may think, "I don't want to deal with it." Yet, in the service of personal evangelism, there needs to be *intentionality* and *availability* to develop redemptive relationships with people.

In our self-centered world, intentionally engaging in redemptive relationships may seem inconvenient. In contrast, in a Jesus-centered reality such relationships are imperative. And we all have a choice.

As His servants, we are called to follow our King, developing relationships with people who've not yet met Jesus.

Sowing Seeds

Earlier we discussed sowing gospel seed, referring specifically to sharing God's word with others. In a more general sense, we've also noted that sowing and watering may refer to building relationships with people, praying for them, and serving them. Trust built over time in a friendship is a good thing, providing a healthy relational platform for sharing the good news. When people know you truly care about them and accept them unconditionally, conversations about divergent views can happen, even when those views are spiritual.

As a college tennis coach, working with the same guys day after day, I developed some close bonds. There was lots of time in the van on road trips, at tournaments, over meals, for conversations to take place. If you hang out with people long enough, you'll eventually get around to discussing most topics, including religion.

I would share my faith with our players in context of the tennis team environment. On occasion, I did Bible studies with players, both on campus and during road trips. Sometimes I gave Bibles as presents to graduating seniors who hadn't yet met the Savior personally. Although I never witnessed any of our players receive the Lord during my time coaching at East Tennessee State University, I can say that I planted lots of gospel seed.

While coaching at East Tennessee State I earned a master's degree in physical education. During my first year at the University in 1991, I became friends with another graduate student, Ruston, an MBA student. Ruston, whose home was India, had a religious background in Zoroastrianism, an ancient Iranian religion. Having never known someone who subscribed to this religion, I asked him about his beliefs and practice.

I learned that an adherent to Zorastrainism believes in a Creator God, known as Ahura Mazda. I also learned that for Ruston to get to heaven in his religion, he had to do good works. During graduate school, Ruston and I shared many meals together. We also enjoyed music and conversation. It was in context of our friendship that I was able to share the uniqueness of Christianity and the claims of Christ. And although he didn't become a Christian while we were in graduate school, Ruston did accept a Bible I gave him. We stayed in touch, as he settled in the United States. A few years after graduate school, Ruston shared with me that he'd become a Christian. We're still friends today.

Remember, in one sense our role as His servants is to sow gospel seed. Take comfort in knowing evangelism is a process and our role is to simply be faithful in what God calls us to. So strive to be faithful and flourish where God plants you.

Relationship is the platform to love people, to serve people, to pray for people... and to share the gospel in word as God opens up doors.

A Relational Reality Check

While personal relationships are natural platforms to share the good news, it's possible to be insulated and isolated from non-believers.

We all have a sphere of influence, which is a group of people with whom we have regular contact. Within this sphere of influence there are various levels of relationship. Yet as we serve the King, He may want us to take the next steps in reaching out to those who don't yet know Christ.

All of us are in one of three places when it comes to unbelievers in our sphere of influence:

1. You have many personal relationships with unbelievers.
2. You have few personal relationships with unbelievers.
3. You have no personal relationships with unbelievers.

Where do you see yourself? It's not as if God is keeping a relational tally on you. Personal evangelism is not about numbers—it's about our heart. Do we have a heart that breaks for the lost and a desire to be a witness? It may be you only have one personal relationship with someone who has not yet met Christ, but that individual may be the one person God wants you to love, serve, pray for, and be a light to. We can't witness to *everybody*, but we can witness to *somebody*.

God wants us to develop intentional relationships with others so we can serve them, love them, pray for them, and ultimately share with them the "truth that sets men free."

A practical move for us is to ask God to show us what steps we are to take next with people in our lives. Perhaps it will be to ask a neighbor over for a meal. It may be asking an associate, classmate, or co-worker out for coffee. Maybe you don't know any non-believers you can befriend. If so, then your next step is to ask God to bring a non-believer into your life for the purpose of befriending.

Before personal evangelism takes place, a personal relationship must be in place.

Raising the Banner

A banner is a flag or other piece of cloth bearing a symbol, logo, slogan, or other message. It communicates allegiance to a group, cause, or country. In the context of evangelism, raising the banner is simply communicating to others that we're followers of Jesus. The prophet Isaiah was commanded to raise a banner and exalt His voice (Isaiah 13:2). Banners not only tell people who you represent, they also attract attention.

Would you agree or disagree with the following statement? "Many people who know me are aware that I'm a Christian." The answer to that question can tell us much about our personal witness.

Raising the banner is essential to our gospel testimony, yet how and when we do that varies. While we always want to live in the state of urgency because people need the Lord, we also want to be sensitive to the fact that incarnational relationships are fluid, organic, and take a life of their own. In other words, we need to be sensitive to God's leading, being flexible in how and when we raise the banner.

There are lots of ways to let people know we're followers of Jesus, but this usually happens in context of relationships. Allow the Holy Spirit to open the door of opportunity and be sensitive to His leading. Everyone in our sphere of influence needs to know we're a follower of Jesus.

Certainly when we're intentional about developing a relationship with someone who doesn't know the Lord, this issue of communicating we're a Christian comes to the fore. When we enter into personal relationships with people for the purpose of being a light for Christ, they may or may not know that we are followers of Jesus. And the question arises: How do we raise the banner? Or in other words—How and when do we make them aware that we are a Christian?

Good question.

Here's one I wouldn't recommend: "Oh, by the way, did I mention that I'm a born-again, purchased with the blood of the Lamb, cleansed from sin, delivered from bondage, sold-out follower of the

King of Kings and Lord of Lords, Jesus Christ?"

Seriously though, we've acknowledged that effective evangelism is Spirit-led and God has a singular ability to move our conversations from the secular to the sacred. We'll discuss witnessing conversations a little later. But for now, asking God how to best raise the banner in a particular circumstance or relationship is certainly a good prayer. There are various ways to communicate you're a follower of Jesus.

While coaching my son's Little League team for two years, I prayed in Jesus' name before every game. And this was a city league, not a Christian league. Asking someone if there is anything you could be praying for is another way to raise the banner. Few people will be offended by that statement. You might have a Bible or something overtly Christian in your workplace. You could wear t-shirts with overtly Christian messages. I have one that I wear on occasion and it raises quite a few eyebrows. It's a Jewish star with this phrase in big letters: Smile, Jesus Loves You.

As we've learned, God calls each of us to walk by faith and go where He calls. Developing redemptive relationships is an adventure. It's an adventure that requires intentionality, availability, and willingness to get our hands messy.

So if you need to raise the banner somewhere or to someone in your sphere of influence, be creative and ask the Lord for help. For people need to know we love Jesus.

The Testimony of Love, Joy, and Peace

Have you thought of your personal relationship with the Lord as having an impact on your witness? I would imagine in terms of what you say or don't say or do or don't do—yes. But what about in terms of simply "being"? By that I'm referring to our unspoken and undemonstrated witness.

Let me be more specific. As servants of the King, our testimony has the potential to be radiant in beauty as we reflect the Lord through the manifestation of the fruit of the Spirit. "But the fruit of the Spirit is love, joy, peace, longsuffering, kindness, goodness, faithfulness, gentleness and self-control" (Galatians 5:22).

Now people may quibble with our words, but there is no denying the power of a joyful countenance on the servant who loves Jesus. I don't know what else to call it except the "Jesus look." You may have your own expression.

The "Jesus look" is what someone sees in a faithful believer, one who exudes the "Joy of the Lord." That joy can only be produced by Him, not our circumstances. This is the fruit of the Spirit described in Galatians 5.

Case in point: Many years ago while I was a tennis coach in East Tennessee, we had a gentleman named Mike who regularly played in our tennis tournaments. On other occasions I'd see Mike at the tennis courts where I was giving private lessons. Mike always had a smile on his face and his joy was contagious. It was a powerful testimony and one that caused me to take notice.

One day I was teaching a tennis lesson and Mike was playing on an adjacent court. This was the day I was going to "confront" him. I had to know. If my theory about Mike being a believer was wrong, then I would have to throw the whole "joy of the Lord" theory out the proverbial window.

I walked to him and said, "Mike, I want to ask you something."

He strolled over with that same joyful expression on his face. "Yes?"

I just blurted it out. "You love Jesus, don't you?"

He grinned even more. "Yes, Yes I do."

"Good. I thought you did because you exude the joy of the Lord."

How's that for a blunt, direct confrontation? The fruit of the Spirit can be quite powerful in our witness to others. Whether we realize it or not people are always watching.

The book of 2 Corinthians tells us that we are living epistles. An epistle is a letter, and as such, it is read. Paul wrote to the believers at Corinth, "You are our epistle written in our hearts, known and read by all men: clearly you are an epistle of Christ, ministered by us, written not with ink, but by the Spirit of the living God, not on tablets of stone but on tablets of flesh, that is, of the heart" (2 Corinthians 3:2-3). The implication is that people are always watching and reading us. And not only our words and deeds are in play, but also our countenance.

I'm a big fan of the movie, *Monsters Inc.* My wife Lori and I like watching it with our children, Elijah and Shoshanna. One of my favorite characters is Roz. In this animated comedy, Roz is the ever watching and listening secretary who keeps things in the Scare Factory in order. There are a few scenes in the movie where she reminds one of the factory workers, named Mike Wazowski, played by Billy Crystal, that she's watching. In fact, she reminds him on more than one occasion. "Wazowski, I'm watching you. Always watching."

Whether we realize it or not, people are watching you and me. Always watching.

At the University of Florida in the mid-1980s, before my salvation experience, I ran into Matt on campus. He grew up in my neighborhood. I remembered two things about Matt: he was an awesome drummer, and he got into lots of trouble. I hadn't seen him in a few years, but the moment I saw him I could tell something was different, very different.

He had a peaceful countenance, and the tone of his words was also filled with peace. Matt shared with me that he'd become a Christian. He said he was recording a Christian concert at a local TV station and wanted to know if I wanted to hang out.

I said, "No thanks", and went on my way. In all honesty, his peaceful countenance freaked me out. It scared me, because it was powerful and unique. I didn't understand it. And, at the time, I didn't want to understand it.

While we should aspire to know Christ intimately and experience and express the fruit of the Spirit in abundance, the response of others to that expression will be mixed. People may be attracted to or repelled by it. The countenance of God's glory in a person may evoke fear. That was certainly the case after Moses had spent forty days with the Lord on Mount Sinai. Upon coming down, the Israelites were afraid to come near Moses because his appearance had changed (Exodus 34:29–30).

When the light of the Lord shines through us, there will be a response. People will either be attracted to or repelled by the light of Christ in us. Matt's testimony of peace impacted me. Initially, I was repelled by the power of that countenance, but looking back on the event I can now see that it was a seed planted in my life—a seed that indicated there was something unique about Jesus and about knowing Him.

Imagine going to your local mall and doing a one-question survey, asking people this yes-or-no question: "If you could experience abundant love, joy, and peace in your life, would you want that?" Very few would say, no. I wonder what the response would be if you added this follow up: "What if I told you that Jesus was the key?"

As we strive to serve effectively in His court, remember that the love, joy, and peace we express is a powerful testimony to those who are watching. May each of us be a living epistle that's a compelling read to the Rozs and others in our life. Because they're watching... always watching.

Friend Not Foe

Personal relationships are the means by which we engage in the service of personal evangelism in the court of the King. In those relationships we can love people, serve people, pray for people, and share the gospel message with people. In the Kingdom of God there are no foes, just friends. So step up, step out, and lean in to those relationships for the purpose of being a light for Christ.

"Let your light so shine before men, that they may see your good works and glorify your Father in heaven" (Matthew 5:16).

Chapter 9
Training Session

SPIRITUAL MUSCLE MEMORY
"You shall love your neighbor as yourself" (Matthew 22:39).

WARM UP
When you think of your neighbor, whom do you think about?

PRACTICE DRILLS
What will it take for you to build relationships with unbelievers for the purpose of showing and sharing God's love?

How will you deal with the inconvenience and sacrifice of getting involved in intentional relationships for the purpose of witnessing?

As you reflect on your relationships, how well are you relating evangelistically?

As a "living epistle " what do you think your life is communicating to others?

What do you want your life to communicate to others?

What are your experiences, if any, with people who powerfully manifested the fruit of the Spirit in some way? Were you a believer or not at the time? How did it make you feel?

MATCH TIME
What next steps will you take in order to deepen an existing relationship, such as inviting him or her out for a meal or coffee?

If you don't have a personal relationship with an unbelieving friend, ask the Lord to bring an unbeliever into your life to befriend.

Pray, "God, grow my witness with gentleness and respect in my dealings with unbelievers. Help me love my neighbor more as myself."

EXTRA TRAINING

Luke 19:1-10.

Chapter 10

Serve, Return, Rally

So, then, my beloved brethren, let every man be swift
to hear, slow to speak, slow to wrath.

James 1:19

A rally in tennis is a string of shots ending in a point. A rally begins with the serve and return of the serve, followed by a series of shots until the point is won by one of the players. A typical rally lasts between ten and thirty seconds. But rallies can be atypical. If you watch or play tennis, you understand no two rallies are alike. Sometimes they seem to take a life all their own.

The longest rally in professional competition was a 643-stroke battle between Vicki Nelson and Jean Hepner on Sept. 24, 1984, at a tournament in Richmond, Virginia.

For tennis enthusiasts, the longest rally in a major championship occurred during the 1978 French Open final, when the legendary Swede Bjorn Borg shared a remarkable 86-shot rally with Guillermo Vilas of Argentina.

For those interested in such records, others in non-competitive situations have had rallies numbering in the thousands that lasted hours.

Tired yet?

The interesting aspect of the rally (in singles) is it takes place between two people and as we've mentioned, can take a life all its own. The rally is unique to time, place, and participants.

The witnessing conversation is much like the rally in tennis: two people going back and forth, not rallying with racquets and tennis balls, but with words. The back and forth occurs through the basic mechanics of questions, listening, and speaking.

No two rallies are alike. Each is unique. Nonetheless, there are patterns and ways of navigating a rally in a functional manner, where the "end-game" will hopefully result in a healthy conversation about spiritual things.

Healthy spiritual conversations include two primary keys: questions and listening. Those two actions go hand in hand. When you're in a relationship with someone, conversations are two-way. Ideas go back and forth. One person talks, the other listens and vice versa. This back and forth pattern resembles a tennis rally, although much less strenuous on the body. Yet, it does put stress on the mind and the spirit. Spiritual conversations about the most important issues in life demand engagement of heart, mind, and spirit. They take work, but they are worthwhile.

Questions: The Key to Opening Conversational Doors

"How are you doing?" We hear and use that question all the time. Often the response is, "I'm fine, thank you." But there are times that seemingly benign questions can open deep, meaningful conversations about the most important issues in life and can sometimes lead to the all-important question: "Who do you think Jesus is?"

I used that question as my opener when doing street outreach as a missionary. After asking someone if I could ask them a question, if they said yes, I would ask, "Who do you think Jesus is?" You might be surprised about how many people are thinking about Jesus and will talk to a stranger on the street. As we noted earlier, God is working on the hearts of people all the time, including people in your sphere of influence.

In the context of personal relationships where you have regular touch points with an individual, there is certainly time to ask lots of questions that propel conversations along. Hopefully, at some point you can pose that most poignant of questions: the question of Jesus' identity. Remember, Jesus asked His disciples: "But who do you say that I am?" (Matthew 16:15).

Think about this subtle but powerful difference: Do I want to speak *to* someone or speak *with* someone about spiritual matters? Speaking *to* someone conveys the idea of talking at them and wanting to get your own point across at all costs. In contrast, speaking *with* someone conveys the idea of working together, sharing ideas and thoughts, seeking understanding. Questions provide a great platform for this kind of synergy.

Questions can affirm others. Inquiry communicates that we care about what another thinks, believes, and feels. We Christians are sometimes accused of only wanting to talk and be heard. Yet a winsome and humble witness will include the willingness to listen, and listening will be the result of asking questions.

Witnessing Conversations are a God Thing

Have you ever thought, "I don't know how to start a witnessing conversation." If so, you're not alone. The key is to start with a question. Let me suggest a good opener: "How are you doing?" Simple enough. Nonthreatening. Any questions that start the ball rolling can be productive. It doesn't have to be profound.

Witnessing conversations are Spirit-led. Have you ever had an impactful spiritual conversation with an unbeliever and not really known how it started from the secular and moved to the spiritual? There have been times I've shared this experience with other believers to encourage them and was asked, "How did it happen?" My response: "I don't know."

God has a beautiful capacity to move any mundane conversation from the secular to the sacred and do it in a way that makes us marvel.

To serve others well, it helps to know whom we're serving. And what better way to find out how to serve others than to ask questions and find out how they're doing. Simple enough.

Questions are a powerful mechanism to begin conversations—conversations that can lead to spiritual matters, which can, in turn, lead to the most important question of all: Who is Jesus?

Like a Box of Chocolates

A fascinating aspect about conversations is that they are like a box of chocolates—you never know what you're going to get. But as we've mentioned, we walk by faith, not by sight. So that should be okay.

When conversations are organic and fluid, questions about spiritual things can occur in the natural course of conversation. When we ask questions, active listening needs to follow. When we "lead with the ear," we can learn much about where someone is coming from.

One day I was at Starbucks working on this book and struck up a conversation with a gentleman sitting across from me. He shared with me that he was a professional photographer who'd moved with his wife and kids from California to Tennessee. He showed me some of his work on his computer. He was quite accomplished. Our conversation meandered to snow skiing. I mentioned I'd skied in Colorado a couple of times. He then mentioned a skiing trip to Utah he'd made as a youth with an organization called Young Life.

Young Life is a Christian ministry. I asked him if he and his family attended a local church in town. That question struck a sensitive chord in him. "I don't need the church to have faith," he responded with an emotionally painful expression. That one sentence spoke much to me. This man had been burned by the church or by people in the church.

I choose not to push it and we moved on amiably to something else.

Another time and another day I may have asked him, "Why do you feel that way?" And that would have been fine. I just didn't.

Since God has wired each of us uniquely, the kinds of questions we ask and the timing of those queries will also be unique.

I was trying to find a table at Starbucks on another day. And yes, I enjoyed writing much of this book while hanging out there. As it happened, a gentleman was leaving a prime work area, and I asked him if he was leaving. When he said yes, I posed a question I wouldn't normally pose, but it just came out. "Do you have any spiritual inclinations?"

He smiled. "Matter of fact, I do."

That began a rather personal and deep conversation about spiritual matters. He was more than happy to share a bit of his spiritual journey with me. He said he'd grown up in a mainline Christian denomination and had come to a place where he was now a universalist—a belief that all paths lead to God and everyone goes to heaven. He also said he was not at all averse to talking about Jesus and even attending a Christian church.

Since he had recently moved to the area, I invited him to attend our church and gave him my phone number if he wanted to chat further.

With Gentleness and Respect

The spirit of evangelism should be one of love characterized by gentleness and respect. In principle, asking questions, listening, and responding means to only talk about matters when someone is willing to talk about them. In my years of witnessing in a variety of settings, I've spoken only with people who are willing to talk. If someone doesn't want to talk, then it's good to respect their wishes. For example, if I asked you how much money was in your bank account, and you said, I don't want to talk about that, then gentleness and respect demands I say, "Okay." Pushing you into a corner and forcing the conversation indicates that I don't care about you or respect your wishes, but rather I'm only concerned with ramming my agenda forward. And at that point I think our conversation would become a bit awkward. If someone is not willing to talk about spiritual things or about Jesus, respect them. We can only go where someone allows us to go.

Building a rapport with people is our initial goal. Find points of commonality. Even on the streets of New York City in a moment I could engage a man and simply say, "Yankees or Mets?" New York is a big baseball town and I'm a Yankees fan. Many times they would chime in with the name of their favorite team.

In our everyday encounters with people in our sphere, we have the opportunity to allow relationships to unfold. Rapport and trust can be built. So take the pressure off.

Now, after building rapport and trust, at some point it's fine to test the waters and ask probing questions. Risk-taking is part of the conversational process. Asking questions is part of the risk-taking process. Remember, trial and error is also part of that process and that requires lots of prayer, wisdom, and discernment.

Aside from building rapport with people, the art of questioning helps us take someone's "spiritual temperature." Questions will help us know whether they are open to Jesus or not. If someone is not open to God, then I'm just a guy. What can I do? If someone is not open to talking about spiritual matters, that's okay. It doesn't stop us from loving them, serving them, and praying for them—praying that someday soon they may become open to talking about Jesus.

As I've said, I coached our son Elijah's Little League team for a couple of years. During that time I developed a friendship with one of the officials, Jack, whose son also played. Jack knew I was a minister at a local church. One day at the baseball complex I ran across Jack and he took a moment to share with me how he and his family were attending a local church and he was really enjoying it.

I told him I was glad, then asked, "Jack, how about Jesus? What do you think about him?" A direct question, a probing question, and a risky question. His response, "I don't want to talk about it." And that concluded that line of questioning.

We've talked about gentleness and respect. This means going only where people allow you to go. I could have pressed him. "Jack, why don't you want to talk about Jesus?" But where would that lead? It could easily turn counterproductive.

In our witness we can know that gentleness and respect is always a good play.

Some Basic Starters

The art of witnessing conversations includes the task of posing questions. Here is a short list of questions that can be posed to direct a conversation toward the spiritual:

a. Have you ever thought much about faith?
b. Do you have any kind of spiritual belief?
c. What's your religious tradition?
d. What do you think about God?
e. What do you think about the Bible?
f. Who do you think Jesus is?
g. How do you know what you're believing is true?
h. What do you think God wants from you?
i. Do you think you're a good person? Why?
j. What do you think happens to you when you die?

Questions like these can open doors to spiritual conversations. When people are engaged this way, their answers will tell you a great deal about them. That knowledge will help you witness.

In their excellent book *Conversational Evangelism*, Norman and David Geisler show the benefit of *conversation* over *presentation*. While not disregarding the necessity of being able to present the gospel, they note the importance of adding conversation to our witness. The world we live in has changed. They note: "The rejection of moral absolutes, skepticism and indifference towards truth, and even an increasing intolerance toward those who believe in absolute truth characterizes today's spiritual landscape. Because of these changes many more people are less interested in a simple presentation of the gospel."[11]

As we've noted, evangelism is a process. The Geisler's agree: "We should take the long-term view and leave that person with the desire to continue the conversation."[12]

Respect the process, understand everyone is on a journey, and trust God to guide and lead our conversations. If you've not had much experience in this realm, then it's a great opportunity to trust God. He'll give you the right words at the right time. Conversations and the posing of riskier questions is a process of trial and error. Even when we think we've blown it, it's okay. It's part of the process of learning, growing, and depending on God to use us as His witnesses.

Conversations are organic and fluid and take on many forms. Understand it, go with it, and walk by faith. Pray God would superintend the conversations and allow Him to redeem those moments for His glory.

Listening: The Key to Qualifying Someone

Serving evangelistically in the King's court requires that we listen well. "So, then, my beloved brethren, let every man be swift to hear, slow to speak, slow to wrath" (James 1:19). With the help of our King Jesus, we will listen so as to better understand and better serve others in His court.

In a witnessing conversation the goal of listening is to find out if that someone is open to hearing more about the claims of Jesus. In other words, to "qualify" someone is to take their "spiritual temperature."

More specifically, to qualify someone is to find out two things:

What is their God-paradigm?

Are they open to engaging the truth claims of Jesus and the Bible?

First of all, everyone has a God-paradigm, a view of God and spiritual things. They may be an atheist or agnostic, they may believe in a personal God or vaguely defined supernatural being. Everyone has some view of God and spirituality. Someone's tradition (or lack thereof) and where they are presently may be very different. Questioning and listening helps us understand what someone believes. This understanding will help shape our witness.

As active listeners we will become informed witnesses capable of effectively contextualizing the gospel. The Apostle Paul wrote, "I have become all things to all people, so as to win some to Christ" (1 Corinthians 9:22). In other words, he witnessed to people where they were, which meant he had to first understand their thinking. Remember, when Paul went into synagogues he reasoned with the Jewish people from the Scriptures, something they understood. But on Mars Hill, Paul addressed the Athenians, who were not well versed in the Scriptures, "Men of Athens, I perceive that in all things you are very religious; for as I was passing through and considering the objects of your worship, I even found altar with this inscription, TO THE UNKNOWN GOD. Therefore, the One whom you worship without knowing, Him I proclaim to you:

"God, who made the world and everything in it, since He is Lord of heaven and earth, does not dwell in temples made with hands" (Acts 17:22-24). Paul knew his audience well and his listening skills helped his witness.

At some point we'll want to find out if that someone is open to talking about their God paradigm. Some people may not want to talk about spiritual things. Respect that and pray that someday they will be open to the idea. Continue to love, serve and pray for them, also praying God would move in their hearts and give them a curiosity to find out more.

We also need to find out if they're open to exploring the claims of Jesus and the Christian faith. They will either answer yes or no. If they are open, be prayerful about what info you can share. There are many great books, DVDs and other resources about God that are available. I would recommend resources from the following people: Josh McDowell, Ravi Zacharias, Ray Comfort and Kirk Cameron, Norman Geisler, and Lee Strobel, to name a few. Among websites, books, DVDs, and blogs, there are an abundance of resources to support your witness to those who are open to hearing it.

Be prayerful and discerning about what kind of follow-up material to share. Remember, because personal evangelism is a process, whatever you may share with someone should include follow up time with them to continue the process.

Jesus, the Master Questioner and Listener

In Luke 24 Jesus gives us an example of questioning and listening as He witnesses to the two disciples on the road to Emmaus. In this account Jesus had already been crucified and resurrected. Jesus met these disciples, Cleopas and an unidentified person, as they walked to the small town of Emamaus not far from Jerusalem.

"And they were talking with each other about all these things which had taken place. While they were talking and discussing, Jesus Himself approached and began traveling with them. But their eyes were prevented from recognizing Him" (Luke 24:14-16).

Then we see an ironic twist in verse 18. Cleopas says to Jesus, "Are You the only one visiting Jerusalem and unaware of the things which have happened here in these days?" Cleopas didn't know it at the moment, but he was talking to the only One who did know everything that happened. Notice Jesus' response. He doesn't explain things to them just yet. He simply poses the question, "What things?"

What a paradox. The One who knows all things asking a question of those who don't know, and they who don't know treating the One who does as if He's the only one who doesn't know. Isn't this our own situation at times when witnessing to people? We who know the truth reaching out in love to share with someone who doesn't see it and yet treated by those who don't know as if we know nothing at all. Have you experienced this in sharing the gospel with somebody? Well, the Lord identifies with us.

Jesus doesn't rebuke Cleopas. He simply asks him a question, wanting to hear his viewpoint. The Lord is in the process of leading them to the truth of His identity and one of the ways He does that is by asking a leading question, "What things?"

Cleopas then shares his own perspective about the current series of events. He acknowledges Jesus was a Prophet of God and that He died on a Roman cross.

Why does Jesus ask Cleopas what happened when Jesus is Lord and knows all things? Perhaps we get a hint from the gospel of John where Jesus prays just before raising Lazarus: "Father, I thank you that

You have heard Me. And I know that You always hear Me, but because of the people who are standing by I said this, that they may believe that you sent Me" (John 11:41-42). Just as Jesus prayed aloud for the benefit of others before raising Lazarus, here He asks this leading question for the benefit of Cleopas and the other disciple. He does this in order to help lead them to the truth of His identity. Jesus' question is also an example to us as we qualify where people are at spiritually.

Later in the narrative we read: "And He said to them, 'O foolish men and slow of heart to believe in all that the prophets have spoken. Was it not necessary for the Christ to suffer these things and to enter into His glory?' Then beginning with Moses and with all the prophets, He explained to them the things concerning Himself in all the Scriptures" (Luke 24:25-27).

The narrative comes to a climax when the Lord shares a meal with them and reveals Himself: "When He had reclined at the table with them, He took the bread and blessed it, and breaking it, He began giving it to them. Then their eyes were opened and they recognized Him; and He vanished from their sight. They said to one another, "Were not our hearts burning within us while He was speaking to us on the road, while He was explaining the Scriptures to us" (Luke 24:30-32)?

Questions provide the platform for listening and this is a great start in the witnessing process. Questions also help us understand if somebody is open or closed to spiritual conversation, what their God paradigm is, and a myriad of other important details.

Listen to the Music

Part of the listening process is not only actively listening to what another is saying, but also listening to the Lord who knows exactly what people need when they need it. Walking by faith means we believe God is working in the hearts of people in our midst. As we walk in our daily lives, we should seek how and where God is working and join Him in that work.

While a new Christian in the late 1980s, I was coaching at a tennis academy in Largo, Florida. A college-aged young man named Rick was training at our academy and needed a place to stay for a few days. So I invited him to hang out at my place. In the process of our conversations the topic turned to spiritual things. And no, I don't remember how it got started.

I remember vividly our having lunch at a fast-food restaurant. Rick shared that he wasn't a Christian but had wanted to receive Christ a few times. He said there was something keeping him from receiving the Lord. During our conversation, I could hear secular rock music in the background. In my conversion experience, the dark messages of certain rock and roll music had been a stumbling block to me prior to coming to Christ. I said, "Rick, listen to the music. Do you hear the words?" He said, he didn't.

In addition to listening to Rick, I was also listening to the Holy Spirit. We drove back to my apartment immediately following lunch and I said, "Let's play a game, Rick. Do you like music?"

"Yes."

I mentioned a particular band and asked if he liked them.

"Yes."

The band I mentioned was a very popular rock band in the day. "Good. Let's play a game. I'm going to play a song and I want you to simply tell me what the words are. Forget the music. Just tell me what the song is saying. Okay?"

I got out an old cassette of this particular group I had lying around. In case you're wondering, I hadn't read any book on evangelism and this wasn't a technique I picked up. I simply felt compelled to share this music with Rick .

I played the first song. Very spiritually dark music. I asked him what the words were saying. He was surprised. He shared a few of the lyrics, noting they were not glorifying to God.

"Ready for the next song?" He said he was. The next song was about hell and the Grim Reaper. Again, spiritually dark. "Well, what did that song say?"

Shocked, he shared a bit then said, "Wow, I've never heard those words before."

"Bingo. Exactly. They don't care if you understand or not. But there is power in those words and they're not from God. Ready for the next song?"

The last song I played was about the way to hell That was it. Following that song he realized that this satanically-inspired music was part of this block that was keeping him from receiving the Lord. He stopped right there and prayed to receive Christ.

What did I know about personal evangelism? Very little. Did I know how he would react listening to a little rock and roll music? I had no clue. All I knew was in my experience, Satanically-inspired music played a part in keeping me in spiritual bondage prior to me being set free by Jesus. I thought this exercise might help Rick.

The point I'm making is that listening is two-fold. We actively listen to others and concurrently listen to the Lord, then follow His lead. When we do, our witness will be more effective.

Open or Closed

At any point in a relationship, we want to find the answer to this question: "Are you open to learning more about Jesus?" If they are, then great. If not, continue to love them, serve them and pray for them.

Part of qualifying someone is to actively listen and discern whether someone is sincere in wanting to know more about Jesus and the Bible. Let's be honest. Some people just have a hard time saying no, even no to talking about spiritual things. If you sense someone is hesitant to talk about spiritual things, perhaps you can help by being direct and letting them know it's perfectly fine if they don't want to talk about Jesus. It will save lots of time and energy.

An important question when dialoguing with someone about Jesus is this: "If you find out it's true, that Jesus is who He claims to be and what the Bible claims He is, will you believe in Him?"

The answer to that question is key. I've had many people tell me over the years in so many words, "I don't care if it's true or not. I won't believe." What do you do with that?

In response to the gospel, people have said things like: "It may be true but I won't believe because:

"My father (or mother) will roll over in their grave."

"I'll have to change and I'm not going to change."

"I'll lose all my friends."

"I'm not going to be anybody's servant."

We can certainly dialogue with people who are honest inquirers, but for those who are insincere, don't care, and really don't want to know, it's best to simply let it rest. For there are times people will qualify themselves by saying—"I'm not interested in Jesus."

Dos and Don'ts

In summary, as God opens doors for spiritual conversations with those who've not yet met Jesus, here are a few general do's and don'ts:

Things to do:

    a. Smile.

    b. Strive to actively listen and understand where the other person is coming from.

    c. Keep the conversation going as long as the person is interested.

    d. Find out what they believe about God or spirituality.

    e. Ask them why they believe what they believe.

    f. Find out if they are open to engaging further the truth claims of Jesus.

    g. Show gentleness and respect.

Things to avoid doing:

    a. Don't assume people know anything about Jesus, the Bible and Christianity.

    b. Don't get into a debate. We're not trying to win an argument.

    c. Don't give people too much information. Leave them wanting more.

    d. Beware of quoting a myriad of Scriptures.
    e. Don't forget the gospel message.

In life our relationships are fluid and dynamic. Conversations take on a life of their own and people process information in their own ways. When we have regular touch points with people, there will be opportunities to test the waters and see where people are regarding spiritual things.

We've described "qualifying someone" as a beginning point in the witnessing endeavor. But certainly "qualifying" is also a continual process in our relationships. So as we track with people, continue to ask questions, listen, learn and share as God opens up doors of opportunity.

The art of witnessing conversations provides an ongoing opportunity to depend on God and trust that He can move in the midst of conversations. Pray expectantly, asking the Lord to move conversations from the secular to the sacred and always be ready with a word or words aptly spoken. In this we find the grace and strength to rally and rally well in the court of the King, keeping the end game in mind—to glorify the Lord.

Chapter 10
Training Session

SPIRITUAL MUSCLE MEMORY
"He said to them, 'But who do you say that I am?'" (Matthew 16:15).

WARM UP
How do you feel and what do you think when you hear the concept "witnessing conversation?"

PRACTICE DRILLS
What has been your experience with "witnessing conversations?"

In your personal witness, how have you used questions, if at all?

In your experience, have you understood evangelism primarily as more talking or more listening? What shaped that understanding?

How can you understand where someone is coming from (belief, worldview, etc.) in order to be a more effective witness?

Why is it important to listen to the Lord in the midst of witnessing to others?

MATCH TIME
Find someone in your sphere of influence to converse with where the goal is simply to ask leading questions and learn where he or she is coming from.

Ask God to grow your ability to actively listen and better understand others, especially in the area of personal evangelism.

Ask the Lord to help you better listen to Him as you witness to others.

EXTRA TRAINING

Study Luke 24:13-35

Chapter 11

A Winning Point

A man has joy by the answer of his mouth,
and a word spoken in due season, how good it is.
Proverbs 15:17

Apoint in tennis is the smallest subdivision of the match, the completion of which changes the score. A point can consist of a double fault by the server, in which case it is won by the receiver; otherwise, it begins with a legal serve by one side's server to the receiver on the other, and continues until one side fails to make a legal return to the other, losing the point.

Okay, okay. A bit dry, I know. So much for technical definitions.

Since this is a book that I hope illustrates the positive, let's talk about winning points, not losing points.

How do you win a point in tennis? Such a simple question, yet one with a myriad of answers.

We've previously mentioned Pete Sampras's devastating serve and Andre Agassi's scintillating service return, but there are lots of strategies for winning a point: patience, aggression, staying back, coming forward, playing the percentages, etc. Chris Evert's success came through her consistent play from the baseline (backcourt), while Martina Navratilova's winning strategy employed coming forward and hitting winning shots with the volley (from the front court).

Ultimately, you want to put the ball into the court one more time than your opponent. If you do you'll win the point. Put the ball in play one more time than your opponent enough times and you will win the match.

Playing, coaching, and watching tennis for decades has shown me one thing about winning points: they come in all shapes and sizes. The commonality is that a winning point is unique to the situation of the moment.

In tennis, winning points is the key to defeating your opponent. In evangelism, making a winning point is a key in "winning" over the one with whom you're having a conversational rally.

In tennis we talk about "having an answer," a winning counter-strategy to the strategy the opponent is employing. "Having an answer" for the challenge your opponent presents is a key to winning points and ultimately winning the match.

Having an answer is a critical element in the evangelistic endeavor. The answer is not a strategy to win points in order to win a match. Rather, it's a "word aptly spoken" in order to appropriately deal with questions and objections regarding the Christian faith.

As we've noted earlier, one of the keys to confidence when entering the court for a tennis match is preparation. That's why day after day we drill, work on all the shots, simulate point situations and play practice sets and matches. Experience helps and the only way to get experience is to play the game.

I grew up playing junior tournaments in the scorching Florida heat. One of the pillars for success in Florida junior tennis would be fitness, because you could lose by wilting in a long match. For me, fitness was a strength. I was in great shape. I was a workout fiend. I ran, lifted weights, practiced hard. I was rock solid and fit as a fiddle. In high school, I worked out virtually every day. Although I lost tennis matches, it was never because I ran out of gas. I could go hard all match long. The only way I attained that level of fitness was to train regularly.

Part of our preparation in serving in His court is being prepared to answer objections. And there's no question about it, they will come. For our purposes let's use objections and questions interchangeably since both require useful answers.

One of the fears we noted earlier was the fear of not having a good answer to a question. Well, fear not. Know you don't have to have all the answers. All you need to know is where to get them. It is also okay to say, "I don't know. That's a good question. Let me get back to you."

While a missionary to my Jewish people in New York City, I met regularly with an orthodox Jewish man in Brooklyn named Aaron. I'd go to his apartment once or twice a month and share the claims that Jesus was the Messiah. One day Aaron raised a very intimidating objection. He said Jesus couldn't possibly be the Messiah due to the curse of Jeconiah. What did I know about the curse of Jeconiah? I had been exposed to it before in my missionary training, but couldn't recall any kind of cogent response at that moment. What's a missionary to do? I'm supposed to have all the answers, right?

No worries. I simply told Aaron, "That's a good question. I'll look into it." It so happens I was familiar with the foremost Jewish apologist in the world, Dr. Michael Brown. He had written the five volume set, *Answering Jewish Objections to Jesus*. Dr. Brown covers every conceivable objection and question that could be raised from a Jewish perspective. I found a biblical response to Aaron's statement and shared it the next time I saw him.

Now I can't say that changed Aaron's position on Jesus—it didn't. The point is there are answers to objections.

There are many great resources available as we seek to provide answers to people's questions. Books like Josh McDowell's *Evidence that Demands a Verdict* (vols. 1 & 2) and *Who Made God and 100 Other Difficult Questions Answered* by Norman Giesler are two prime examples.

When thinking about how to answer objections, I want us to establish some ground rules:

When qualifying a person, we need to find out if they're open to the answer. The $64,000 question we need to raise is this: Are they genuinely interested in getting an answer to their question and if so, are they prepared to deal with the answer?

There are consequences for anyone who engages in honest inquiry about Jesus and the Christian faith, the most profound consequence being: "What will you do if you find out that Jesus is exactly who He claims to be?" In other words: "If God shows you the gospel is true, will you believe in Jesus?"

When someone raises questions or objections, we need to determine whether that person is sincere or insincere. The honest inquirer is searching for the truth. The insincere may raise questions as sport because they want to blow you off or make you squirm. This is where listening and qualifying apply. For the insincere, there's no need to waste your time scrambling for answers.

I've often asked people, especially my Jewish people this question: "Is there any possibility Jesus is the Messiah?" If they say no, we're done. What can I do? I'm just a guy. If a person has already made up their mind, fine. If they say maybe, my next question is: "Are you interested in finding out?"

Find out if their question or objection is sincere. Do they really want to grapple with a response? If so, proceed. If not, continue loving them, serving them, and praying for them as we've noted.

Additionally, when we think about answering questions and objections regarding our faith, it's important to define terms.

Hebrews 11:1 states, "Now faith is the substance of things hoped for, the evidence of things not seen." Therefore, faith is substantive and based on evidence. I have, many times, been accused of having blind faith. Many Christians have. Yet our faith isn't blind. God has given us many reasons to believe. First and foremost, the tomb is empty. And that truth claim upon which our Christian faith rests or falls begins with this historical fact.

Coffee Shop Answers to Standard Objections

There are a limited number of strategies employed in an attempt to win a tennis match. One can play with aggression or patience. A player may camp out at the back of the court or may rush the net to finish points off quickly. There are power players, whose style of play is to hit the ball hard and harder. In contrast finesse players want to beguile you with placement and touch. And then there is a combination of all of the above—having a balanced game, being able to employ various strategies and execute various shots. This is reserved for more advanced players.

When a tennis player can identify what style of strategy is being employed, they can make necessary adjustments and begin to win points. In our Christian witness there are only a limited number of basic objections to our faith and being able to identify what they are will help us be able to produce winning points. As anticipation is important in tennis, so it is important in our witness. As we anticipate objections and questions about the Christian faith, it will help to have what we might call a "coffee shop" response. In other words, when posed, do we have a simple answer that can keep the conversation centered on the topic at hand? If we do, we can move the dialogue along. If not, then as we've stated, it's okay to say, "That's a good question. I'll get back with you."

Here are five common objections to Christianity and a coffee shop answer—an initial response that moves the conversation along:

1. What about the atrocities Christians have committed?

My standard response to above question is this: People have done terrible, awful things in the name of freedom and justice for millennia. Does that make freedom and justice bad? Of course not. Yes, people have done terrible, awful things in the name of Jesus and under the banner of Christianity. But don't throw the baby out with the bathwater. Jesus never did any of those things. Sinful, wicked people perpetrated those acts, of which they will give an account to God. In fact, Jesus was about love, so much so that He taught, "Love your enemies, bless those who curse you, do good to those who hate you, and pray for those who spitefully use you and persecute you." So, any person who perpetrated such acts, Christian or otherwise, was certainly not following the teachings of Jesus.

As an aside, I relate to this very well. As a missionary to my Jewish people, I would often be verbally attacked by people who said in so many words, "How can you tell us about Jesus when Christians have been persecuting Jews for 2000 years?" If you want to read a powerful book on this topic, I recommend the book *Our Hands Are Stained With Blood* by Dr. Michael Brown.

2. It's narrow-minded to think Jesus is the only way to God.

Every world view, religion, and philosophy is by definition exclusive and excludes other truth claims. That's what makes a truth claim a truth claim. Yes, Jesus claimed he was the only way to God (John 14:6). Such a claim is either totally true or totally false. The reality is the exclusivity argument doesn't hold much water. The beauty of the gospel is the inclusiveness of its message: "For God so loved the world that He gave His only begotten Son, that whosoever believes in Him should not perish but have everlasting life" (John 3:16). If Christianity is true, then we must accept all of Jesus' teachings. He doesn't give us the option to pick and choose.

As a follow-up, we might ask, "Well, tell me how you think we get to God and why you believe that?" Remember, defending one's worldview, or giving an *apologia*, is not exclusive either. In other words, the one you are speaking with must be held to the same standard, defending what they believe and why they believe it.

3. Being a good person is all that really matters.

First of all, what is the definition of a "good" person and who makes that determination? Jesus Himself said, "No one is good but God" (Matthew 19:17). The Bible is very clear about the goodness of man and his ability to be good: "There is none righteous, not even one. There is none who understands, none who seeks God. All have turned aside, together they have become useless. There is none who does good, there is not even one" (Romans 3:10-12). The gospel is about acknowledging we are not good. The Bible calls us sinners and that sin separates us from God. The Bible says God is good, He is righteous. In His goodness He sent His Son to die for our sins and rise again so we could be brought into a right relationship with God. So, the gospel is not about being good. It's about trusting in the One who is.

4. What about those who've never heard about Jesus?

But you have. Who do you think Jesus is? No one has ever remained lost who wanted to be found. Jesus promises all who seek will find (Jeremiah 29:13, Matthew 7:7-8). People always have been and always will be responsible for the light they have received. And if people are searching for light, God will reveal light. Jesus said of Himself, "I am the light of the world" (John 8:12). In fact, God has revealed Him in the creation as Creator, His invisible attributes are clearly seen, so they (anyone who rejects God) are "without excuse" (Romans 1:20).

Remember, we're not skirting the issue to this deep question. Rather, an initial response should make the issue personal, not philosophical.

5. The Bible is filled with errors.

Can you please show me one? The Bible claims to be God's Word. Jesus claimed it to be true (John 17:17). Apparent contradictions in the Bible are just that, apparent. In fact, as a piece of ancient literature, the Bible is more credible and reliable than any other. And if you're interested, I'd be happy to provide you evidence that supports the veracity, credibility and reliability of the Bible.

As a follow-up, you might ask, "Do you want to know if the Bible truly is God's Word?" Again, we want our response to be personal.

Here are a few other basic objections that require thought, an initial response, and other resources that further discuss the subject:

- "Christians are hypocrites."
- "Christianity is a crutch."

- "If God is so good, why is there evil?"
- "Why is there suffering?"
- "If there is a hell, why would a loving God send people there?"

And we could go on.

As you think through these and other questions, you'll develop your own coffee shop responses—good beginning points to a conversation.

As we've stated, there are many excellent resources that can provide in-depth responses to honest inquirers. One book I'd recommend is *Who Made God? And Answers To 100 Other Tough Questions Of Faith* by Ravi Zacharias and Norman Geisler.

Don't run from questions and objections. Expect them, prepare for them, and know where to get answers. And when providing answers, do so with a spirit of love characterized by gentleness and respect.

Patience: Always a Winning Play

I met an unsaved Jewish man named Nick through his Gentile girlfriend, a believer. When I first contacted Nick, he told me his biggest issue with believing in Jesus as the Messiah was the resurrection. Nick, who was in his sixties at the time, was open to a conversation. If he found it to be true, he would have no problem believing in Jesus. Well, an eighteen-month spiritual journey ensued. There were periodic phone calls, studying the Scriptures with Nick, and articles I sent his way. He was also doing his own research into the matter. The process culminated one day with a phone call. Nick told me over the phone that he was satisfied with the evidence for the resurrection, believed it to be true and had trusted in Jesus as Messiah. That was a happy day. But it took eighteen months—that's a journey.

Some people's journey to faith takes many years. Because our faith is based on evidence and substance, we want to be prepared to give a reason for the hope that is within us.

Don't fear objections and questions when they arise. Simply qualify the one posing them as sincere or insincere. If they're sincere, provide them answers, praying along the way that the Holy Spirit would help them to see, understand, and ultimately believe in the One who is the Answer—Jesus.

A Trophy of Grace

In my nine years of coaching college tennis, some of the sweetest memories I have are those moments when we clinched a conference championship. It was a moment in time—a moment of culmination. Tennis is a process. Winning is a process. Winning a conference championship is a culmination of that process, and it is a sweet end to a journey that begins with the first team meeting when school begins in the fall and ends with one last swing of a tennis racquet that had been swung thousands of times over the course of a year. Culmination. Exaltation. Relief.

All along the journey there are obstacles. There are ups and downs. Victories and defeats. Key moments that help define the direction of a team. Then with one player, one point, one magical moment, it all comes together—victory! Game, set, match, and championship.

I have many sweet memories as an assistant tennis coach at East Tennessee State University. During my six-year tenure as the Men's Assistant Coach we won three regular season Southern Conference Championships and three Southern Conference Tournament Championships. It was a privilege to play a role, my role, in the effort of those teams. The moments following that final point in which a championship is clinched is, although unrehearsed, somewhat of a victory procession.

And part of that victory procession is when the team is acknowledged and the trophy awarded, received, and raised. That's a lot of fun.

As a servant in the King's court, we do the King's bidding. Sometimes in the process of serving in His court, He may give us an opportunity to join a celebration—a victory procession.

This party is a heavenly party that even the angels partake in.

When a trophy of His Grace is ushered into the Kingdom, He may allow us as His servants to be a witness in the proceedings.

Make no mistake. It's His prerogative, it's all of His doing, and if we are privileged to be present at this gala, we should shudder in humility and at the same time exclaim His praises.

This party, you may wonder—what might it be?

Salvation—of course.

The Bible describes the event. "There will be more joy in heaven over one sinner who repents than over ninety-nine just persons who need no repentance" (Luke 10:7). "There is joy in the presence of the angels of God over one sinner who repents" (Luke 10:10).

Our Role and God's Role in Leading Someone to Jesus

As His servants it's important for us to understand who is leading whom to Whom. When we think about leading someone to Jesus, it is God who ushers the sinner into the Kingdom. We can and do play a role, but ultimately we need to remember, God is sovereign.

What is our role? What is God's role?

In John 15:16, Jesus said to His disciples, "You have not chosen Me, but I have chosen you, and ordained that you should go and bring forth fruit..." God is the one in charge. He is the one who is doing the calling, the choosing, and the leading. We can and should draw encouragement and incentive knowing this.

The consequence in our witness is that if God is in control, it means that we can't turn off somebody the Holy Spirit is turning on.

Practically speaking, we don't lead anyone to Christ. Rather, He uses us as His instruments to direct to Himself those people in whose hearts He is at work. It's the Holy Spirit who initiates illumination, conviction, repentance, and confession unto faith. Our job is to work with those God is working with and help them confess Him openly to actualize salvation. This is seen in Romans 10:9-10. "That if you confess with your mouth the Lord Jesus and believe in your heart that

God has raised Him from the dead, you will be saved. For with the heart one believes unto righteousness, and with the mouth confession is made unto salvation." What a blessing to be allowed to take part in this process.

It's important to note that people have free will and must exercise their choice to believe in Jesus. Therefore, you and I can't manipulate, cajole, pressure, or intimidate someone into believing in Jesus. If we could, their conversion would be disingenuous and our witness inappropriate.

Communicating the Main Points

Essentially there are two paths that lead to a decision to trust in Jesus. Generally theologians call them the Damascus Road and the Berean Road. The Damascus Road involves an encounter with the living God and subsequent conversion. The Apostle Paul is a prime example of the Damascus Road experience in Acts 9. The Berean Road (see Acts 17:11) involves a process of searching the Scriptures and results in the intellectual realization that Jesus is who He claims to be, followed by a heartfelt need to repent and trust in Him to be reconciled to God. An example of a Berean Road experience is the case of the Ethiopian eunuch who was studying the Book of Isaiah when the Spirit of God caused his path to intersect with Philip (Acts 8:26–40).

Some people come to faith after studying the Bible extensively, others come with very little Bible knowledge. The manner in which a person comes to faith is often a combination of both roads. It's not necessary for someone to understand all the intricacies of the Christian faith to be saved. What is needed is an understanding of three essential concepts:

Sin

Sin is defined as unrighteousness or anything that violates God's Holy standard. Sin is not only expressed in action or thought; it's also our very nature. We are born with a sinful nature, and as such are called sinners. Therefore, we sin because we're sinners, not sinners because we sin. As sinners, we need to be saved from our sin (Romans 3:23).

Salvation

Saved *from* what? From the consequences of sin, which are judgment, wrath, and eternal separation from God in hell. Saved *to* what? To victory and abundance in this life and eternal life with God in the life to come (Romans 6:23, John 10:10).

Savior

Sin is a terminal disease. It kills everyone. Everyone is infected with it and Jesus is the only effective cure. He took our sin upon Himself, freeing us from the curse of sin's consequences. But we must appropriate that cure by trusting in Jesus.

If they aren't ready to trust in the Lord, ask them what is keeping them from making that decision. Here are two pitfalls to avoid when leading a person to Christ:

1. "I never promised you a Rose Garden." We've mentioned this before, but it bears repeating. Never mislead a person into thinking that believing in Jesus will make them healthy, wealthy, and free of life's troubles. Do let them know He is the solution to their greatest need, the need to be forgiven and reconciled to God.
2. "The Pitfall of Pressing." It's important to know when to encourage someone to trust in Christ and when to let up. Don't come on too strong. Be prayerful. Never coerce a person to make this most important of decisions. If someone is close but not ready, it may be appropriate to encourage them to pray that God would reveal Himself to them and show them whether or not the gospel is true.

When a person moves to a point where they believe the gospel, it's appropriate to ask them if they're ready to trust in Christ. If they say yes, you can lead them in a prayer to receive the Lord. Here's a sample prayer: "God, I know I have sinned against you and I want to turn from my sins. I believe you provided Jesus as payment for my sin and I believe He rose again on the third day. With this prayer I receive Jesus as my Savior and Lord. Thank you God for forgiving my sin and cleansing me from all unrighteousness. Help me to follow you all the days of my life. Amen."

It's not the prayer that saves. The prayer is an affirmation of faith in what God is already accomplishing in a person, bringing them out of the Kingdom of Darkness and ushering them into the Kingdom of God, making them a child of God. Salvation is a gift of God.

When someone makes a decision to trust in Jesus, it's imperative that they find a local church and begin the discipleship process. Be there for them as a fellow child of God, praying with them, reading God's Word with them and helping them develop spiritual disciplines. Remember, trusting in Jesus is not the end, but rather the beginning of their walk with the Lord.

Be Encouraged, Be Faithful

I think it good at this point to note that most Christians in their lifetime won't be present to witness or participate in that event of conversion where the Holy Spirit brings someone out of darkness and ushers them into the light of the Kingdom, making that person a child of God. The reality is this: God simply calls you and me to be faithful to sow and water however He leads us—in loving, serving, praying for, and proclaiming truth to people. If He allows us to be present and participate in that salvation event, praise God, but if not, praise God.

So, don't feel guilt and shame because you've never led someone to Christ. In all my years as a Christian, I've had the privilege of being a witness and being a vessel God used to help someone enter the Kingdom, but only on a limited number of occasions. My heart's desire is that I would be a faithful witness in whatever way my King wants me to be. If I'm present during this moment in a person's journey of faith, I certainly rejoice. Yet, to be faithful to fulfill whatever role God calls me to in the evangelistic process is my highest aspiration as a witness for Jesus.

Who led me to Christ? God did, and He used servants like Herb, Greg, Matt, Steve, and others as His witnesses to demonstrate and proclaim His Good News. I thank God that they were faithful in loving me, praying for me, sharing the gospel with me, and challenging me to seek God.

The first few times I heard the gospel I was resistant. Most people are. Research indicates that in general, it typically takes several exposures to the gospel message for a person who does trust in Christ to make that decision.

It's like a pitcher of water. Someone coming to faith in Jesus does so when the pitcher is full. And you and I have the privilege of pouring a drop or two in that pitcher. Then others come along and they add water—a drop here and a drop there until the pitcher overflows. This is the mystery and beauty of the gospel.

And God is faithful.

Jesus said, "I will build My Church and the gates of Hades shall not prevail against it." I believe Him. And the wonder is He uses His servants to participate in His Kingdom building program.

Now, that's a winning point.

Chapter 11
Training Session

SPIRITUAL MUSCLE MEMORY

"A man has joy by the answer of his mouth, And a word spoken in due season, how good it is" (Proverbs 15:17).

WARM UP

How has fear of not having an answer to questions hindered your personal witness?

PRACTICE DRILLS

What are some of the most common objections to the Christian faith you've experienced in your Christian walk?

In what ways do you need to be equipped to provide an adequate response to questions?

Have you ever experienced someone objecting to your faith who was just trying to "rub you the wrong way" or simply trying to "brush you off?" How did you feel? What was your response?

If someone said to you, I want to receive Christ, what would you do? How does knowing your role and God's role in leading someone to Jesus shape the perspective and engagement of your personal witness?

MATCH TIME

Take a few minutes and identify what you've are learned about about qualifying and whether a person in your sphere who has questions or objections is sincere or insincere.

What steps do you need to take in order to grow in your personal apologetics?

Seek the Lord for guidance as people pose questions about the Christian faith.

EXTRA TRAINING
Study Acts 8:26-40.

Chapter 12

Game, Set, Match

To everything there is a season,
A time for every purpose under heaven.
Ecclesiastes 3:1

W hat was the greatest season in tennis history? While there have been many dominant seasons, there's no real way to definitively pick one over another.

Since John McEnroe is my all-time favorite player, I'll choose his 1984 season. Johnny Mac's 1984 campaign is certainly considered one of the best seasons ever. That year McEnroe won both Wimbledon and the US Open. His performance in the finals at Wimbledon, where he beat Jimmy Connors 6-1, 6-1, 6-2, and the US Open, where he defeated Ivan Lendl 6-3, 6-4, 6-1, were particularly dominant. His record in 1984 was 82-3, that's 82 wins and only 3 losses, a winning percentage of 96%.

Although McEnroe reached new heights during that amazing 1984 season, he didn't stop playing. It was simply another season on his journey, as he played until 1992 before retiring from the professional tour. He put that 1984 season to rest and prepared for the next season.

Just as tennis seasons come and go, so goes our walk with the Lord. We put one season to rest and prepare for the next season of life. For there is "a time for every purpose under heaven" (Ecclesiastes

3:1) and "He has made everything beautiful in its time" (Ecclesiastes 3:11).

The Elements of a Successful Season

There are parallels between a tennis player's season and our seasons of life in the court of the King. Consider these three parallels between a tennis player's successful season and a Christian's successful season serving in the court of our King:

Preparation. Tennis pros understand the things that will make them successful. This includes an understanding of how to train—drills, practice sessions, practice matches, nutrition, mental training, stretching, strength conditioning—and then how to put those elements together to give them the best chance at success. Once attaining "success," the tennis players in the middle of their careers don't just retire and rest on their laurels—they continue to the next match, the next tournament, the next season. For you and me in the court of the King, the first step of preparation is to understand the process; to understanding evangelistic principles.

Practice. The tennis player executes the game plan for success, following the training program. After mapping out their game plan, they execute it for success. This involves the competitive schedule where they engage in actual competition and test themselves to see where they are. For us, that is the application of evangelistic principles. In short, this is the engagement of non-believers in our sphere of influence.

Progression. For a competitive tennis player, this refers to the personal growth that takes place as a result of preparation and practice. They strive to reach new heights in their career and continue to improve, to build their legacy, and to grow as athletes. Their victory is in the journey, not simply in reaching a destination. For our witness, that progression is simply growth—growth in our understanding and application of the biblical principles for personal evangelism, and ultimately, our growing closer to Jesus in the process.

What is the win? Victory for the tennis player is winning matches.

Our victory is to better understand the principles and more intentionally engage in the process of evangelism through application of those principles.

And as we mentioned before, "success in witnessing is simply taking the initiative to share Christ in the power of the Holy Spirit and leaving the results to God."[13]

Reviewing the Main Principles

As in sport, so it is with personal evangelism—repetition is a key to success. As we conclude our discussion, it's worth a look back at the foundational principles that should define our evangelistic efforts in reaching the lost for Jesus Christ.

The Rules.

In our evangelistic efforts, understanding these three main principles will enable us to engage in the personal evangelistic endeavor: evangelism is a process, evangelism is a heart issue, and evangelism is a team thing.

The Process. Jesus' parable of the soils in the Gospels (Luke 8:4-15, Matthew 13:1-23, Mark 4:1-20) sheds light on this reality. We're called to sow gospel seed, which is the Word of God, and that takes time. The "soil" is the condition of a human heart, as Jesus explained, and is where the seed lands. As one Bible commentator notes, "The soils do not represent individual moments of decision as much as a lifelong response to God's Word."[14]

Think about it in physical terms. A farmer sows seed—that's an event. It rains one day—that's another event. The sun comes up day after day and feeds that seed—those days are individual events. It rains another day—that's an event. And so on. The Apostle Paul adds: "I planted, Apollos watered, but God gave the increase" (1 Corinthians 3:6).

The Heart. May our hearts for the lost be aligned with God's heart as we engage our sphere of influence. "But sanctify the Lord God in your hearts, and always be ready to give a defense to everyone who asks you a reason for the hope that is in you, in meekness and fear" (1 Peter 3:15).

Central to God's redemptive plan in delivering people out of bondage to sin into freedom in Christ is His desire to seek and save the lost. In Luke 19:10 Jesus said, "The Son of Man has come to seek and to save that which was lost." That was you and me at one time, and now those people we interact with on a daily basis in the marketplace who have yet to trust in Jesus.

The Team. Jesus said to his disciples at the beginning of His earthly ministry, "Follow me and I will make you fishers of men" (Matthew 4:9). And just before ascending to heaven at the end of His earthly ministry He stated, "Go and make disciples of all nations... and I will be with you always" (Matthew 28:19, 20).

One of the mysteries of the gospel is that while God is all-powerful and is the author of salvation, He chooses to use people like you and me to bring others to Himself. We, the church, are integral to His redemptive plan. In fact, the Lord commands us to be actively involved in His redemptive work.

Be encouraged. We are on the winning team. For Jesus said, "I will build My Church and the gates of Hades shall not prevail against it" (Matthew 16:18).

Watching the Ball.

The most important message we bring to a lost and dying world is the gospel message. The Apostle Paul said, "For I delivered to you first of all that which I also received: that Christ died for our sins according to the Scriptures, and that He was buried, and that He rose again the third day according to the Scriptures" (1 Corinthians 15:3-4).

As we share the gospel, keep in mind that it is God alone who is the author of salvation. It is the Holy Spirit who convicts sinners of their sin, opens their understanding to the truth of the gospel, and does the work of regeneration in a person who puts their trust in Christ.

The Opposition.

The devil and his minions oppose our evangelistic efforts in the of midst a spiritual war: "For we do not wrestle with flesh and blood, but against principalities, against powers, against the rulers of the darkness of this age, against spiritual hosts of wickedness in the heavenly places" (Ephesians 6:12).

In addition, Satan seeks to keep unbelievers blinded and bound by lies, lest they be set free by believing in the truth of the gospel: "But even if our gospel is veiled, it is veiled to those who are perishing, who do not believe, lest the light of the gospel of the glory of Christ, who is the image of God, should shine on them" (2 Corinthians 4:3-4).

We are also opposed from doing the work of evangelism by the "old man" that resides within each of us—namely our flesh. The Apostle Paul encourages us to walk in the Spirit, "I say then: walk in the Spirit, and you shall not fulfill the lust of the flesh. For the flesh lusts against the spirit and the spirit against the flesh; and these are contrary to one another, so that you do not do the things that you wish" (Galatians 5:16-17).

But take heart. We have the victory in Christ. "Now thanks be to God who always leads us in triumph in Christ, and through us diffuses the fragrance of His knowledge in every place" (2 Corinthians 2:14).

Our Equipment.

"For though we walk in the flesh, we do not war according to the flesh. For the weapons of our warfare are not carnal but mighty in God for pulling down strongholds, casting down arguments and every high thing that exalts itself against the knowledge of God..." (2 Corinthians 10:3-5). Our standard "equipment" for engaging in the battle of personal evangelism includes the Word of God, the Spirit of God, the Gospel, and prayer. As we appropriately utilize these God-given resources in our evangelistic efforts, we can be the witnesses for Jesus He intends for us to be. "And God is able to make all grace abound toward you, that you, always having all sufficiency in all things, may have an abundance for every good work" (2 Corinthians 9:8).

A Well-Balanced Game.

The two pillars of biblical evangelism are proclamation and demonstration. We are to share the gospel in word. "Proclaim the good news of His salvation from day to day. Declare His glory among the nations, His wonders among all peoples" (Psalm 96:2–3). We are also to demonstrate the gospel through good works."For we are His workmanship, created in Christ Jesus for good works, which God prepared beforehand that we should walk in them" (Ephesians 2:10). The proclamation is imperative in evangelism, as "faith comes by hearing and hearing by the Word of God" (Romans 10:17). Yet, in our personal relationships, the most impactful personal witness is someone who loves people in both word and deed. In general, we said that truth without love lacks authentication and love without truth lacks explanation. So tell them about God's love found in Jesus Christ, and show them what God's love in Jesus looks like.

The Game Plan.

Jesus, even from His youth, was about "His Father's business" (Luke 2:49). You and I are also to be about the Father's business. Specifically, seeking out the lost as Jesus did in order to love them and share the gospel with them. Jesus said, "For the Son of Man came not to be served, but to serve and to give..." (Mark 10:45). As His followers we are called to do the same. And as we follow Jesus, we should strive to focus less on *our* business and more on *His* business, serving others in Jesus' name with the hope that they would come to a saving knowledge of the Savior. As we serve the lost, we also want to be aware of how God has transformed our story, being ready to share our testimony with those in our sphere of influence.

Walking By Faith.

"For we walk by faith, not by sight" (2 Corinthians 5:7). Engaging in the personal evangelism process is a faith venture to be sure. And part of the deal is you don't really know how things will go when you go. Yet, when He calls us to go, we are to follow. Personal evangelism is a great adventure. When God called Abraham to leave everything he knew to go to the land of Canaan in Genesis 12, Abraham simply obeyed. Just before His ascension into heaven in Acts 1:8, the resurrected Jesus told the disciples they were going to be His witnesses to the utter ends of the earth, although they had never left the Holy Land. In one sense we are the result of their faith. So go where He leads, for "without faith it is impossible to please God" (Hebrews 11:6).

Facing Fear.

Fear is real in various areas of life, including the realm of personal evangelism. Courage is doing what God calls us to do in spite of our fear, not in absence of fear. When it comes to facing the fear of sharing our faith, we must grapple with this question: "Is their salvation more important than my safety?" The answer to that question will shape our evangelistic efforts, because the evangelistic process is risky business. Yet, the risks of rejection and misunderstanding are worth the reward of planting gospel seed that may contribute to the entrance of one person into God's eternal Kingdom. And those, my friend, are risks worth taking. Jesus told us, "There will be more joy in heaven over one sinner who repents than over ninety-nine just persons who need no repentance" (Luke 15:7). "For God has not given us a Spirit of fear, but of power and love and of a sound mind" (2 Timothy 1:7).

Friend or Foe?

"You shall love your neighbor as yourself," Jesus said in Matthew 22:39. Friendship is the platform by which we engage in personal evangelism, for personal evangelism is personal. Yet we know that relationships are hard work and messy. There are people who need Jesus that we may not jibe with. But God may call us to befriend someone in order to establish an incarnational redemptive relationship for the purpose of being a light for Christ. Yes, even "difficult" people need Jesus. People are never our foes in the spiritual. In fact, the Lord states this about our enemies: "But I say to you, love your enemies, bless those who curse you, do good to those who hate you, and pray for those who spitefully use you and persecute you" (Matthew 5:44). Additionally, Jesus said in Matthew 25:40, "Whatever you've done to the least of these, you've done it unto me." So seek the Lord's face on this matter of relationships, pray for incarnational relationships with the purpose of being a witness, and follow Him where He leads. For people need the Lord.

Serve, Return, Rally.

Witnessing conversations are a two-way street. They require us to ask timely questions and listen with an attentive ear. That takes practice. We need to be prayerful and patient in our personal relationships. Pray for open doors, pray that God would move conversations from the secular to the sacred, and be willing to take risks in asking leading questions of a spiritual nature as God leads. There are many great resources to continue study in this area and many opportunities to engage in conversations with people. For in our sphere of influence, where we see people on a regular basis, we have a built-in advantage of many opportunities to converse, build rapport, and develop trust. This relational component allows time and margins to process what's been shared. Hopefully, as God provides opportunity, we can discuss with those we know and love the most important of questions, namely, "Who is Jesus?"

A Winning Point.

Answering objections and questions is key in the evangelistic process. For people who are sincerely searching for truth need adequate answers to questions and objections on their journey. So we need to provide answers. "A man has joy by the answer of his mouth, And a word spoken in due season, how good it is" (Proverbs 15:17). It's not that we need to be ready to have an answer on the spot, but we should know where to find answers to any questions raised. By God's grace, we may have an opportunity to participate in the beautiful event of someone trusting in Jesus Christ and entering the Kingdom of God. And remember, when someone believes in Jesus, that's not the end of the journey; rather, it's the beginning. So be sure to begin the discipleship process with that person. Get them plugged into a local church or congregation and walk with them, helping them understand and engage in the basics of walking as a child of God. Introduce them to prayer, Bible study, fellowship, service, and, yes... evangelism.

Evangelism by the Book

The account of the salvation of the Ethiopian eunuch in Acts 8:26-40 illustrates well some of the foundational principles discussed throughout the book.

Verses 26-27 highlight availability and obedience to the Lord. "Now an angel of the Lord spoke to Philip, saying, 'Arise and go toward the south along the road which goes down from Jerusalem to Gaza.' This is desert. So he arose and went."

Verses 28-35 highlight questions, listening, and answering questions. The Spirit tells Philip to overtake the Ethiopian's chariot. When Philip arrives, he sees the Ethiopian man reading from the prophet Isaiah. He asks (v. 30), "Do you understand what you are reading?" The man responded (v. 31), "How can I unless someone guides me?" Philip walks through this open door quite nicely. The Scripture is open to Isaiah 53:7-8. In verse 34 the Ethiopian asks, "I ask you, of whom does the prophet say this, of himself or some other man?" Philip provides an answer (v. 35), "Then Philip opened his mouth, and beginning at this Scripture, preached Jesus to him."

Verses 36-38 highlight salvation with Philip fulfilling his role. The Ethiopian eunuch, after hearing the gospel from the Scriptures, says to Philip (v. 36), "What hinders me from being baptized?" Philip responds, "If you believe with all your heart you may." Notice Philip qualifying the eunuch, finding out if he believes the gospel before baptizing him. He's not pushy at all.

The eunuch states (v.37), "I believe that Jesus Christ is the Son of God." Philip then baptizes him. Hallelujah.

Next Steps

Competitive tennis players work on footwork in a variety of ways. To properly navigate the tennis court requires the player practice every conceivable action. There is side-stepping, split-stepping, running, stopping, starting, cross-overs, scissor-kicks, ready position, sliding, and bouncing that keeps one's weight on the toes and ready to go in an instant.

Why? To put oneself in the appropriate position to hit whatever shot is required on the court.

As servants in the court of our King, we must practice another kind of footwork—steps involving our personal witness to others. And the question for you is—what are your next steps?

Certainly God has one or more steps for you in this great adventure called personal evangelism. And the beautiful thing is, He knows what they are and they are good. Another beautiful thing is whatever they may look like, He will enable you by His grace and through the power of His Spirit to take them.

In our walk with the Lord, because our Christian life is dynamic and ever changing, there is always a next step.

One of the paradoxes of the Christian life is since He's in the process of conforming us into the image of His Son, the never-changing God is helping us grow as we experience the ever-changing process called sanctification.

The next steps may be big or small. But it's not about the distance; rather, it's the direction. Are you moving toward the Lord and His will for you in this area?

Perhaps they're baby steps. You can do this.

Perhaps they're big steps. Maybe this is one you've been wrestling with for a while and it's time to say, "Yes Lord."

Is it praying more faithfully for a missionary or praying regularly for those in your life who need Jesus? Is it praying God would bring an unbeliever into your life? Perhaps you're compelled to take the next steps in an existing relationship as God leads. Sharing a cup of coffee, sharing an evangelistic video or book. Maybe it's seeking to serve someone through an act of kindness or service.

Maybe the next step would be to read or study some other books by Christian authors as you seek to grow in your witness.

Many Christians think the evangelistic process is like trying to jump on a speeding freight train—way too hard and way too dangerous. The reality is that the freight train is moving slowly, almost crawling. God is the Conductor and He wants us to get on. It doesn't matter if you know where it's going. The Conductor knows. The important thing is deciding to get on.

All I can tell you is that it is going to be an adventure... and it's going to be okay.

Will you get on? It just takes a step. A step of faith.

Welcome to the next season of your life. "To everything there is a season, A time for every purpose under heaven" (Ecclesiastes 3:1).

Yes, he has made everything beautiful in its time and now is the time for you to act.

So, onward servant of Jesus our King. His court is before you...

Chapter 12
Training Session

SPIRITUAL MUSCLE MEMORY

"To everything there is a season, A time for every purpose under heaven" (Ecclesiastes 3:1).

WARM UP

Reflect and record how God is moving in your heart in the area of personal evangelism as a result of reading this book.

PRACTICE DRILLS

What principle do you most need to focus on in your personal witness?

What are the top three priorities you will commit to in order to grow in your personal witness?

MATCH TIME

What are the next steps God is calling you to engage in during your journey to being a more effective witness?

Who is it that God wants you to be praying for and serving?

Ask God to help you grow to be more intentional, available, and relational in your witness to others.

EXTRA TRAINING

Study Ecclesiastes 3:1-11

About the Author

Christianity is Jewish!

I know, I know! I'm stating the obvious! Or perhaps that's a revelation to you. Whatever your response to that statement, know that my views about that statement have changed dramatically. At one point it was completely irrelevant. Today, that comment plays a major role in who I am as human being.

Growing up in a Reform Jewish home in St. Pete, Florida, I attended synagogue, and at age 13 went through Bar-Mitzvah which means "son of the commandment" and is a ceremonial rite of passage when a Jewish boy becomes a man. Though we were culturally and socially very connected to the Jewish community, we were not a particularly religious household.

Growing up I believed in God as far back as I can remember and had some sense that He *knew* me. In high school I sought fulfillment in athletics and academics, as I was a state-ranked tennis player in Florida and an honors student. But accomplishment didn't fulfill the longings of my soul.

In college at the University of Florida I got involved in the party scene. This didn't satisfy me either. In fact, I was that young person walking in quiet desperation – empty and walking without a plan for life.

My earliest memories of people sharing Jesus with me go back to my college years. But, I consistently rejected any conversation about Jesus and turned down invitations to church, Bible studies, and Christian concerts. Then a good friend named Greg, who was a Christian, challenged me. He said, "Do you know who you are and do you know where you're going when you die?" I had no idea how to begin answering those questions. In fact, they sent me into an existential crisis of sorts. God used that crisis as a catalyst in my life, as I began searching for truth in 1985.

At that time I embraced neither my Judaism nor any other religion, but began to examine different philosophies and world religions for answers to life's biggest questions.

I searched for something I could believe in, something that would fill a void I felt in my life that accomplishment or earthly pleasures could not fill. My search culminated in the fall of 1987 when a stranger on a plane challenged me to ask the God of Israel if Jesus is the Messiah. I took his challenge, crying out to God as I knew Him to show me the truth about Jesus.

He did, and in December 1987 I trusted in Jesus. I believed for the first time that He died for my sins and rose again from the dead so that I could be forgiven. Knowing Messiah *was* and *is* the greatest thing that's ever happened in my life, but it's not been easy being a Jew for Jesus.

Something profound occurred in my life as a new Christian: I made a discovery that was quite astonishing to me at the time. As I began studying the New Testament, I learned about the Jewishness of Jesus. I also learned all the writers of the New Testament were Jewish with the possible exception of Luke. I thought to myself, "Christianity is Jewish!"

In one sense the gospel narrative is simply a Jewish debate among Jewish people about the true identity of a Jewish man, Jesus. And the story takes place in Israel. What could be more Jewish than that?

The Impact of the Holocaust

My father immigrated from Bonn, Germany with his family in June 1939, escaping Nazi persecution. My paternal grandparents and my young father escaped with help from an SS Agent in the Nazi party. The agent, a friend of my grandfather's from WWI, falsified immigration papers enabling my father and his parents to escape to Belize, where they lived for two years before moving to Daytona

Beach in 1941. None of my father's remaining family in Germany survived the holocaust.

Professional Tennis Coaching

I picked up my first tennis racquet at the age of 9 and from the ages of 12 to 18 I competed in the Florida junior circuit, earning my highest state ranking of #20 in the boys 16-under singles division. It was my main sport, though I loved playing many sports. After graduating from the University of Florida in 1986, I began coaching under my high school coach, Billy Stearns, at his academy in Seminole, Florida. I trained world class juniors, college and professional tennis players. During my 20s and 30s, I was a professional tennis coach who loved my outdoor "office" and working with people. I came to East Tennessee to pursue my Master's Degree in 1991, and joined the coaching staff at East Tennessee State University under Head Coach Dave Mullins. Coach and I worked together for 9 years, and I taught private lessons and clinics on the side with a faithful client base.

Stepping Away from the Racquet

As I grew as a Christian, my desire to share this good news with my Jewish people also grew. I wanted them to know that yes, it is Jewish to believe in Jesus, for He is the Jewish Messiah and Savior of the world. I prayed for God to make an opportunity for me to share the gospel with fellow Jews.

In 1989 a family friend passed on a pamphlet from Jews for Jesus, a missionary society committed to sharing Messiah with the Jewish people. Before receiving this newsletter I thought I was alone, the only Jew who believed in Jesus.

After a few years of receiving the newsletter, I decided to serve for a 6-week summer outreach with Jews for Jesus. In the process of applying, I learned about *The Liberated Wailing Wall*, Jews for Jesus' mobile evangelistic music team. This team shared the good news of Jesus through music, drama, and testimony, mainly at churches and at

Christian colleges. They also would engage in street evangelism in big cities and on college campuses. After much consideration and prayer, I went ahead and applied for the music team as well.

In the plan of God, a 6-week short-term mission trip turned into a two-year full-time ministry commitment. In June of 1997, I left Johnson City, Tennessee with no more than a book bag, a 29-inch hard-shell suitcase, and a guitar. Everything else I left in storage. I boarded an airplane, flew away and entered a life-changing adventure!

In December of 1997, before my team left for our tour of ministry, we recorded a messianic praise album called, *This is Jerusalem.*

In January 1998, my team of 6 members and I loaded our gear onto a 40-foot fully equipped tour bus which would become our home on the road. I co-led the traveling music team on our journey around the United States and Canada from January 1998 to March 1999. At the end of our North American tour, we embarked on a 2-month world tour doing ministry in England, South Africa, Australia, and Hawaii.

Needless to say, after doing over 500 presentations in a myriad of diverse church settings and evangelizing around the world, my life was forever changed.

During my tour, I courted a beautiful woman named Lori, and at the end of the tour I asked her to be my wife. We were married in the fall of 1999 and two years later God blessed us with our firstborn son, Elijah.

Ministry in the Big Apple

In 2002, I was accepted onto vocational missionary staff with Jews for Jesus. My family and I packed up our house and moved to New York City in January of 2003. Arriving in the Big Apple, we moved into our apartment in midtown Manhattan. Shortly after arriving in New York City, Lori and I learned that we were expecting our second child, a daughter.

In Manhattan, I trained under some of the brightest and most gifted missionaries and Bible teachers including the late Dr. Jhan Moskowitz, who taught me much about preaching, and Dr. Jack Meadows, my private theology professor. Following the training, I was ordained, and then continued on as a missionary in the heart of New York City through mid-2009.

Pastoral Service

I have been a member at Grace Fellowship Church in Johnson City, Tennessee for over 20 years, first coming to the church in 1993. Grace Fellowship has been the most influential church in my Christian life. It was here I learned to function in a local body of believers. The church supported and sent me out on both my 2-year and 6-year missionary stints with Jews for Jesus. Just prior to leaving for New York City in January 2003, I sat under staff pastor Tim Bowers in a six month resident's program where my main responsibilities included developing a seeker-sensitive, gospel-centered Bible study.

After leaving staff with Jews for Jesus in 2009, I served as Missionary-in-Residence for a year before becoming the full-time Local Outreach Pastor. In that role I developed and directed various community outreach programs and missions activities, trained missions teams, taught classes and preached on a number of occasions.

Larry Stamm Ministries

I am a Jewish Christian in love with Jesus the Messiah and the Word of God. God's work in my life to this point prepared me to launch Larry Stamm Ministries in early 2013 with the full support of our Board of Directors, my family, and my home church. My experience since 1997 in witnessing around the globe to people of all walks of life has uniquely qualified me to teach and share biblical principles with others and to help them share their faith more confidently.

More and more Americans are avoiding the church and an increasing number of both irreligious and religiously unaffiliated no longer have friends who are Christians. We can't afford to isolate ourselves, or to stop reaching out to our co-workers, neighbors, classmates, and others. The onus is ever more upon individual Christians to share Jesus in the marketplace: at the coffee shop, with your neighbor or coworker, your classmates and others with whom you have everyday contact.

Larry Stamm Ministries exists to make the gospel of Jesus a confident topic of conversation for every Christian. We provide classes, one-on-one evangelism coaching and teaching that connects the dots between the Old and New Testaments in order to inspire Christians to press on in fulfilling the Great Commission.

Connect with Larry

Larry Stamm Ministries
Post Office Box 1072
Jonesborough, TN 37659

Phone: 423-426-5055

E-mail: lsm@larrystamm.org

Twitter: https://twitter.com/LarryStamm

Facebook: https://www.facebook.com/larrystamm.org

Author website: http://larrystamm.org/

Vimeo Video Channel:
https://vimeo.com/channels/larrystammministries

ENDNOTES

[1] *"'Nones' on the Rise"*, pewforum.com, *October 9, 2012,* http://www.pewforum.org/2012/10/09/nonesontherise/

[2] Bill Bright, *Witnessing Without Fear: How to Share Your Faith with Confidence,* (Nashville: Thomas Nelson,1993), 67.

[3] Jerram Barrs, *The Heart of Evangelism,* (Wheaton, Crossway Books, 2001), 103.

[4] Earl D. Radmacher, gen. ed, *The NKJV Study Bible,* (Wheaton, Tyndale, 2007), 1610, comment on Luke 8:11.

[5] *"How Michael Chang defeated Ivan Lendl at the 1989 French Open,"* Steven Pye; That 1980s Sports Blog; May 21, 2013 (http://www.theguardian.com/sport/that-1980s-sports-blog/2013/may/21/michael-chang-ivan-lendl-french-open-1989)

[6] Ibid.

[7] Paul McElhinney - *"Martina Navratilova vs Chris Evert Head to Head and Rivalry,"* Steve G Tennis Blog November 12, 2012, http://www.stevegtennis.com/2012/11/martina-navratilova-vs-chris-evert-head-to-head-and-rivalry/

[8] Arron Chambers, *Eats With Sinners,* (Cincinnati: Standard Publishing, 2009), 14.

[9] Ibid., 15.

[10] Ibid., 14.

[11] Norman Geisler and David Geisler, *Conversational Evangelism,* (Eugene, OR:Harvest House Publishers, 2009), 18.

[12] Ibid., 24.

[13]Bill Bright, *Witnessing Without Fear*, 67.

[14]Earl D. Radmacher, *The NKJV Study Bible*, 1610.

Made in the USA
Monee, IL
30 July 2021